VIRAL PODCASTING

A PROVEN PROCESS
TO EARN A 6 FIGURE INCOME
FROM YOUR SHOW

Written by Kerry Lutz

Foreword and Contributions by Valerie Geller, author of Beyond Powerful Radio

VIRAL PODCASTING: A Proven Process to Earn a Six Figure
Income From Your Show
Copyright © Kerry Lutz 2016
Published by Rushmore Holdings LLC

ISBN-10: 1540641260
ISBN-13: 978-1540641267

What the experts are saying about *Viral Podcasting*...

I had the honor of teaching Kerry how to launch his podcast back in July 2011. Since then, Kerry has produced an incredible amount of content and found some truly unique methods for growing his audience. I'm thrilled to see that he has written a book to document some of the valuable lessons that he's learned along the way.

–Cliff Ravenscraft
Founder & CEO at PodcastAnswerMan.com

"The advent of the internet has fundamentally changed media forever. Newspapers have been replaced by blogs. Radio replaced by podcasters. Television and movies replaced by YouTube. However, not only has the format by which we take in media changed, but the internet has put the ability to create movies, shows, music, and literature in the hands of the common man. No longer do aspiring artists, singers, authors, musicians, or actors have to beg for permission from oligopolistic record studios, radio stations, newspapers, or elite New York publishing houses. All one needs is a laptop, a microphone, internet access and an idea and they can sell themselves directly to the world. It has created a virtual Wild West v 2.0 where any ambitious and determined individual can make it, and Kerry Lutz is one such man.

In his book "Viral Podcasting" Kerry Lutz gives the hopeful new-coming pioneer a much-needed road map to the world of podcasting. He shares his trials and errors, mistakes and successes, resources and mentors. He goes through the philosophical and psychological requirements to become a successful podcaster, as well as the technical requirements including everything from hosting services to mic booms. If you are looking to become a podcaster there is no better book available. "Viral Podcasting" is simply a "do-your-homework-must" before you invest your time and energies into starting a podcast.

There is no guarantee, of course, that you'll become as successful as Mr. Lutz. To be a serious and successful podcaster takes hard work, serious determination, creativity and time. But it is a guarantee his book will make that process not only infinitely easier, but much shorter as well. Hopefully someday, like Kerry, you'll be sitting on a beach in Florida, a café in Cuba, or a casino in Monaco while podcasting from the balcony of your hotel. And the first step to that path is reading "Viral Podcasting."

–Aaron Clarey
Host of "The Clarey Podcast"
Fan of the "Financial Survival Network"

As a podcaster with 12 years of experience, over 3,000 episodes and substantial financial success, I thought I'd seen it all—or most of it. However, after reading Viral Podcasting, I came to understand that there's even more to the field of podcasting. The techniques outlined in Kerry's book have enabled me to substantially increase audience size to over 100k additional downloads per month. Buy the book and apply the techniques he's developed. You have nothing to lose but those low download numbers and your podcast may go viral too!

–Jason Hartman
  www.JasonHartman.com

"I wrote my #1 bestselling book PODCASTNOMICS in 2014 to educate people on the nuts and bolts of podcasting: what it is, why it's a worthwhile business undertaking, how to get started technically, and how to monetize effectively.

Three years later, **Viral Podcasting** picks up where **Podcastnomics** left off. Up-to-date and state-of-the-art, Kerry shares his podcast success story, and it leaves readers feeling inspired to give podcasting a shot - whether as a listener, host or producer.

—Naresh Vissa

Table of Contents

Foreword

So you've thought about doing a podcast, but aren't sure where to start, how to get help or who to talk to? Viral Podcasting is "one man's podcast success story." If you're interested getting started—creating a podcast, ideas on how it can make money and how to build and grow your podcast audience, ultimately to build and enhance your brand? This book will give you a starting point. But first, a podcast needs to do five things: Entertain, Inform, Inspire, Persuade and Connect with people.

Several years ago—a call came in from a guy who wanted to know if he 'had what it takes" to be a professional broadcaster. He was a lawyer, working in real estate and had a few other irons in the fire. But he loved radio, and hosting a talk show was his dream. He asked: "Do I have what it takes to successfully host a talk show?"

He called me, as over the years, I'd built any number of successful radio shows in a broadcast career culminating in a job as program director of WABC in New York. There, finding and developing on-air personalities was key. I went on from there to train and coach broadcasters—working with more than 500 radio and TV stations all over the world—first developing, then teaching methods to help broadcasters become more powerful communicators and to get, keep and grow audiences. I now coach podcasters. ALL based on the same principles: Tell the Truth, Make it Matter and NEVER be BORING when creating content for audiences in a medium where unique content is king.

If you've ever given a talk, or hosted a podcast or show—you may have discovered, it's a little harder than it appears. The curse of our business is that talented people make it look so easy, so you figure, "Anyone can talk, right? How hard can it be?" It's hard. Communicating powerfully and being a powerful storyteller, interviewer and "expert" with a podcast of any kind takes work.

While not everyone is a gifted on-air or podcast personality—ANYONE can improve and learn skills to be a more powerful communicator and storyteller. You can't "teach talent" that's inborn—but if someone has talent, or an area of expertise, or a message, or story to tell, you can learn the skills to do an entertaining or informative show—or podcast.

Those techniques can be found in the book, Beyond Powerful Radio: A Communicator's Guide to the Internet Age (Focal Press 2011). Kerry worked with these ideas and proven techniques from my book and using these techniques, was able to successfully build and launch his podcast, creating unique content in his field of expertise, financial planning and investing (which I probably should say here—I know NOTHING about and must say I am not connected in any way with his content) but when Kerry asked me if he could use my material, and take some helpful sections of my book to use in his new book: Viral Podcasting—I was delighted to say yes.

There are many ways to do a podcast—this is Kerry's story—how he took an idea and helped build his brand and make a living by creating a successful podcast, now listened to by millions of people.

Kerry I am proud of you and hope with this book, that your story will help and inspire others.

Valerie Geller
Geller Media International
Broadcast Consultants/Training
www.beyondpowerfulradio.com
www.gellermedia.com
www.twitter.com/vgeller
EmailValerie@gellermedia.com

Acknowledgements

Like all books, many people make numerous invaluable contributions to helping the author on his path towards success. First there is Professor Sandra Salish, who is responsible for piquing my curiosity about radio in 1976. Then Valerie[*], without whose belief and commitment I would have been lost. Cliff Ravenscraft, for showing me how the podcasting process really worked and making it simple. Pat Flynn, for proving that one can make a living out of online pursuits. Marion, for saying that I couldn't do it and providing me with the opportunity to prove her wrong. To Mike Gazzola, for showing me how much I was truly capable of doing. John Lee Dumas, who showed there were no limits in any endeavor. David Fischer, for being a perfect client. To the late, great Bob Chapman, who taught me about the power of a great guest. Chris Walzek and Robert Ian, who showed me I could do it. Chris Krimitos founder of the Florida Podcasters Association for providing selfless and unflagging support to the community. And finally, I would like to thank Adam Curry and John T. Dvorak, the best in the business.

*Follow Valerie Geller's guidelines at the end of this book for creating powerful radio.

Introduction

What is a podcast? The best definition I've found so far wasn't in a dictionary or taken from some podcasting pioneer, it was on a random tech site, which stated, "Podcasting is the preparation and distribution of audio files using RSS to the computers of subscribed users. These files may then be uploaded to digital music or multimedia players like the iPod. A podcast can be easily created from a digital audio file." Kind of technical, I know, but accurate. All you need is a computer or other device like a phone or the outdated namesake, the iPod, and you can enjoy the virtually endless streams and archived streams of millions of podcasts. Podcasting got its start in the early 2000s. The exact chronology is murky but these three people were key to its creation: Tristan Lewis, Dave Winer and Adam Curry. The term *Podcast* emerged in 2004. The big leap forward came in 2005 when Apple added podcasts to its iTunes music platform.

Without getting into a lot of extraneous history, things moved on slowly from there. Podcasting has evolved, never really taking on traditional radio, but rather waging somewhat of a war of attrition. Radio stations now offer most of their shows in archival podcast form.

Podcaster ranks continue to swell, with more interesting podcasts hitting the market and driving audience expansion daily. With smartphones becoming the norm, with even newer model cars coming pre-configured with smartphone integration, podcasts are getting ever more popular and easy to access.

However, the vast majority of podcasts and podcasters exist unnoticed in obscurity and no one cares. It doesn't have to be this way. Whether you're looking to start a podcast or you're a podcaster who's trying to be heard and just not making your mark on the world, then this book **is** for you.

When I started my podcast in 2011, I had big plans but realistic expectations. I didn't know if anyone really wanted to hear what I had to say, in fact I was pretty certain that there were very few who did. But I wasn't going to let that stop me. If all those other idiots out there could podcast, then so could I. I just needed the technical knowledge to produce and distribute my shows and I would let fate handle the rest.

Thus began my journey becoming a podcaster. There was no guide like this of which you are reading, so I did it my own special way, as has every successful podcaster. But there are certain lessons learned over this time period that can help others to realize their dreams. Unfortunately, for all but a very small minority, the process will not be easy or fast. Unless you have a lot of money to burn or possess a certain measure of celebrity, or just get plain lucky, it's going to take some time and effort. But if you really love what you're doing and you're passionate about it you'll have the best time of your life.

Over the years, before the money really started flowing, I was plagued by doubts about whether my podcasting business could ever be viable. Many times I gave serious thought to just giving up and getting a *real* job, for the first time in my life. The problem was that every time I thought about it, I came to the realization that there was nothing else that I wanted to do. I was making progress, each podcast I did was better than the last one. Finally persistence and the refusal to give up paid off. The show hit breakeven in 2014 and profitability in 2015. Now in 2016 it's full speed ahead!

I decided to write this book to help the existing as well as the aspiring podcaster who have no clear roadmap for success. For the average podcaster starting out today, there are just bits and pieces of a plan. As it stands, you've got to be in this game for at least six months to a year, and a heck of a lot of trial and error to learn the basics of podcasting before it starts to become clear what works for you to garner subscriptions and of course, money. The problem is that by then, if you haven't gotten fed up and quit, you've wasted perhaps a year of time and funds that could have been spent helping you become profitable and making you a better podcaster. Mistakes can be costly so why not make as few as possible? As the quote goes, "A fool can learn from his own mistakes, but it takes a truly wise man to learn from those of others."

There are so many tools and people available to help your show grow. However, ultimately, your show's success depends upon you. Your ability to turn your vision into a successful business will rely upon your ability to take advantage of the numerous opportunities to monetize your podcast. If you're like most podcasters, monetization will not take place until you reach critical mass in terms of listeners and the amount of content you've created. It occurs as a byproduct of the creative process. Quality content is the only way to ensure your podcasting will ever return a profit and then continue to be profitable. You can't hurry monetization along and make it your chief goal. It's far more important that you produce a great show with high production standards, than getting started with five sponsors. Remember, the TV and radio networks can only command the outrageous advertising rates they charge (or used to) because they produce outstanding quality programming. (Yes we can argue about the quality of the latest season's bumper crop of sitcoms, but they are without question professionally produced and have tremendous advertising dollars behind them). In the beginning, before the networks got those outrageous fees, all they had was their high quality content. So don't put the horse before the cart and worry more about sponsors and free perks than doing the best show you possibly can do. However, you may have unique circumstances like a close friend or family member who wants to help you by being a sponsor or maybe the only way that you can do your show is by obtaining a sponsor, then do what you have to do, but never compromise quality.

Just understand that there is a better way and I am going to share it with you. This book isn't going to tell you spend a bunch of money on your podcast, although like any business venture, money can help. It's just a more structured and organized path that will enable you to succeed faster and to learn to avoid the pitfalls and mistakes that sometimes seem inevitable. All the mistakes have already been made, no need for you to repeat them. With a little bit of thought and planning you can go a lot further than you ever thought possible, in a much shorter time period. Who knows, you might even go Viral!

Connecting The Dots

It was the second class of my first day at Pace University in 1976. Speech 101; it was a core requirement for first year freshmen, but what did I need this for? Pace is an urban university that wrote the book on diversity, before anyone even knew what diversity was. Thanks to the miracle of open admissions, kids who could barely speak or write the language were attending college. The school was only too happy to take these kids' money and the government's money, cross their fingers and hope for the best.

Growing up in an affluent Northern New Jersey suburb, I thought I already possessed all the verbal skills I would ever require for attending to life's demands. I didn't really have much of an accent, my diction was decent and I was pretty articulate for a college freshman. Little did I know. Professor Salisch walked into the classroom and the room went silent. She told us to prepare a 2-minute impromptu speech about anything, using certain words and vowels. I still remember some of it today. I spoke about the jaundiced athlete in the White House, Ronald Reagan. It got a few laughs and then she evaluated me. I had an occluded "S" (still do) and my "A's" were a little eastern sounding. She thought I had a bit of an Upstate New York accent (never lived there and neither did my parents), but overall she said I had a beautiful voice and that I could be on the radio.

I was amused and somewhat pleased by her critique, but immediately discarded the suggestion of a radio career. Being a DJ, making $15,000 per year and talking to myself all day, just didn't turn my lights on. This was before the talk radio revolution that would make some show hosts very wealthy celebrities. So instead, I opted for the family business where I felt my future was headed. But the seed had been planted. The thought of being on the radio unconsciously lingered on for decades. It was like a low-grade virus, always in the background, never quite all gone. Over the years, as I would listen to show hosts opine on a variety of topics, I would think, I can do that better, I'm smarter than him or her.

Fast forward to June 7, 2011, a momentous day in my life. That was when I became a full time radio show host and podcaster. As I write these words, it is 5.5 years later, my show and network are popular, approaching 1 million downloads per month and I'm making a nice living off of ad sales, sponsorships and events.

This path has been a challenge the entire way. I've been almost completely on my own. Besides a few technical tomes, there's not much published guidance. There are very few books on how to become a top rated podcaster or media personality. While there are a number of measures of success, it becomes a question of which one to choose, revenue, downloads, Facebook Friends or Twitter Followers.

It's not really a matter of building a better mousetrap and the world beating a path to your door. You could be the finest radio show/podcaster in the world, but if no one knows about it, you will fail.

Therefore, the purpose of this book is to help familiarize you with the technical basics and then move on to the most important and difficult task, building your audience.

I had been a lawyer for 30 years. I had started a number of successful businesses. Yet I was never truly fulfilled in my professional life. So if you're wondering, what would possess a person to give up a successful law career to enter the risky world of media, that's part of the reason. A psychoanalyst might see a less than happy childhood, where I was always left wanting for attention and never fit in with the "in" crowd. Or perhaps it's the desire to be heard, to feel like one is making a contribution to the overall public debate. But most importantly, it is the love of the spoken word, which is truly an advanced art form. There's a real craft to doing talk radio or podcasting, and doing it the right way. The satisfaction and fulfillment derived from podcasting and live streaming is something that I've never come close to in any of my other numerous careers.

The reasons that I've become a media host are many and varied, the fact that I'm the master of my own ship, and I sink or swim based on the quality of the job I do is a refreshing and exciting situation. When I nail a show, it's a real high that keeps me going on to the next one. It's an amazing feeling. It feels as if I have, for however a brief period of time, achieved my life's purpose. I'm doing something that I never believed I could do and that so many others fall short of accomplishing.

Would I recommend podcasting to someone who has an interest in entering the field? It really does depend upon the person, their circumstances and their passion as well as their motivation for considering this work (podcasting). If you're like me and other successful podcasters, it's a calling.

The beauty of podcasting is that you don't have to give up your day job. However, to get really good at it, you must invest a substantial amount of time and a modest amount of funds. The unfortunate part is that achieving proficiency doesn't guarantee you success—whether you measure success by audience numbers or generated income. And the two are not synonymous, audience numbers do not equal income and vice versa.

Building an audience can enable you to monetize your podcast and to achieve your financial goals, the more people in your audience the more opportunity there is for monetization. Some people believe in building audiences gradually, organically, one member at a time. My personal view is that this metric is crucial to your success and to your ability to earn a living off your podcast. Many available courses, while good intentioned, spend far too much time on the technical aspects of podcasting and not enough on the marketing and branding aspects.

According to Rob Walch at Libsyn, one of the largest podcast server sites in the industry, a successful podcast is defined as one that receives 200 or more downloads per episode. **Less than half of all shows actually exceed this threshold.** I can understand that if you're starting from scratch, getting to that 200-viewer level seems like a major milestone, but if you've been podcasting for years, consistently, and you aren't too far beyond that threshold, then you are holding the right book to help you as well.

I Want To Be On The Radio

Growing up in the New York Metro Area during the late 1960s and early 1970s, I witnessed the birth of talk radio. My parents always listened to WNEW AM. Ted Brown, William B. Williams and company spun Tony Bennett, Frank Sinatra, Benny Goodman and many other hits from the past and present. For me, it was boring radio. I wanted to hear the Beatles, the Stones and Led Zep. When my parents would go into a store and leave me in the car, I would immediately change the station to WABC-AM and listen to the latest hits. Two minutes later they'd be back in the car and I'd be stuck listening to Old Blue Eyes once again.

And then, all of a sudden, talk emerged out of nowhere. FM radio had been freed by virtue of the FCC simulcast ban. FM stations could no longer simply re-broadcast their AM sister station's content. They had to come up with their own original programming. Alternative rock stations popped up all over the FM dial and the country. AM started talk radio; the first stations were WOR and WMCA. My parents became voracious consumers of the late Bob Grant (famous for telling callers, "Get off the phone you dummy!"), Leon Lewis, Barry Farber, "Long John" Nebel and others whose names now escape me. It was a non-stop diatribe of everything that was wrong with the city, the state, the country and the world, from the talk show host's perspective anyway.

My friends and I used to make prank phone calls and get past the screener and then mutter obscenities or make crazy statements. One time I found myself debating Bob Grant, about marijuana legalization. I might have been slightly intoxicated and finally he asked me, "Do you use marijuana?" I answered a resounding, "Yes." (Hey this was the '70s.) He replied, "I thought so, you are the best argument for keeping it illegal that I've ever heard." I promptly shouted a string of invectives and was immediately dropped from the line. But I was hooked and knew that one day I would be a radio talk show star.

It should only be so easy. At the present time, all the podcasts that I produce, create and promote are approaching 1 million downloads per month. It's been a long arduous struggle, no not a struggle—a challenge that I have been completely consumed by since that day in June 2011.

Whether you're starting from scratch or have an existing podcast, if you intend to follow me and hopefully surpass my modest success, I wish you the best and hope you will find this book extremely helpful, entertaining, frustrating and relevant.

Best wishes for your success in this incredible field.
Kerry Lutz, Palm Beach County FL, December 2016

It's A Process

Becoming a successful podcaster is a process. There's no single thing you can do that will catapult you to success. Yes there are the Marc Marons, Pat Flynns, Adam Carollas, Leon Laportes and Adam Currys of the world, who seemingly come out of nowhere, garner huge audiences, and effortlessly make multi-million dollar advertising deals, but they are clearly the exceptions.

For the rest of us, if we want to be Viral Podcasters, we need to follow a process. I've reconstructed the process making it as clear and easy as possible. If you follow these simple steps, your odds of success will increase dramatically. And there's plenty of room for you to do it in your own way and style. Many of these steps are optional, some are superfluous and others are just icing on the cake. However, I'm not sure which are unnecessary or which, if any, I would eliminate if I were starting out today. I *do* know that first and foremost, you must treat your podcast as a business. This will force a discipline upon you. Without that discipline, you'll just be relying upon luck and fate to secure your future. And while hope and change may work for some people and professions, it's not going to take you very far in this game. There is no substitute for having goals, acquiring the right tools, having a plan for getting there and making the right investments of time, energy and money. Then add in a little luck and nothing can stand in your way. But if the Podcasting Gods don't smile upon you with overnight success, you'll still be making measurable progress that will keep you moving towards your goals and closing in on the elusive goal that you crave.

Someone once told me that success in life is more about what you don't do than what you do. That's especially true in podcasting. If you're a self-saboteur, you need to eliminate those habits from your life. But getting rid of the negatives is only half the battle. You can't rise to the top in any profession without acquiring success-building skills! If you're a surgeon, getting rid of bad surgical techniques isn't going to make you a world-class doctor. You must learn the state of the art techniques that will make you number one!

It's the same with podcasting. Your verbal skills better be top notch. Comedic skills are important too. You might not be Jay Leno or Jimmy Fallon, but you've got to have a sense of humor and give your audience at least a few chuckles or you're going to bore them to tears. Your style is up to you, but whether you're appealing or you connect is up to your audience. You might be doing this thing for yourself, but your success is going to depend upon the people in your audience and how entertained they are.

Think about the anchor man/woman on the nightly news. Nothing could be more depressing than the state of today's world. And yet they pull it off every night. They keep it moving, conveying the information that you need to know in a manner that informs you, without being totally depressing, at least most nights anyway.

So if you cannot entertain your current audience or future audience, give it up now. I personally believe that everyone has it within them to be an entertainer. The truth is, you're doing it right now. No doubt, your friends find you entertaining; if they didn't they probably wouldn't be your friends. Don't they laugh at your jokes and your stories? Your family no doubt does, if they don't then maybe you should find another family. On second thought that might not be so easy. The point is that you have skills that you are unaware of, have untapped or not fully developed, and chief among them is your ability to entertain.

Storytelling is the way that you refine and develop that skill. As my good friend Wayne Allyn Root says, "Facts tell and stories sell." You must become a master storyteller to make it in this medium. I'm still growing here. The better you can tell a story, the more successful you'll become. NPR is the proof of this concept. While I resent that it is an overfunded governmental recipient of my tax dollars, I cannot deny that they have extremely high production values and that they are master storytellers. That's why they're always getting awards and have a large audience in spite of their biased reporting and ideologically driven agenda that they so vehemently deny the existence of.

Are You Cut Out For Podcasting?

Are you cut out for this? Is this what you really want to do? Are you ready to fully commit? If you want to be successful at podcasting/radio, you can't just casually opt-in and say, "Oh it would be fun to do a podcast." While many people get into it that way, this is a surefire prescription for failure. You've got to make a total commitment. Remember the scene in the movie *Boiler Room*? Ben Affleck is the master sales trainer. He's got the trainees around the table and throws out the keys to his Ferrari. Then he delivers his pitch. "You're going to have to learn this business and work your f--king asses off." That's what it comes down to in podcasting. Success is not going to find you; you're going to have to grab it. You can't just start a show and expect to go viral in one week, or one month. It doesn't work that way. You have a long, and at times lonely road ahead, filled with potholes and very few financial rewards, until you make it. You have to love what you're doing and be totally committed. Otherwise, find something else easier to do like selling life insurance, real estate or automobiles.

What's Your Why, How Do You Define Success?

When you embark upon the podcaster's journey or any other business or career, you've got to know what your *why* is. Mike Gazzola taught me this. It really makes all the difference. Why are you thinking about doing this? When you have the answer to this question, you'll be able to make your plan and have a higher probability of success. For some, podcasting will be a rewarding hobby. For others, they're looking to make it a successful business. Still others are using it as a brand extender or additional marketing tool for an existing, often successful business. Still others are looking for their opinions, thoughts and voice to be heard. Some others just want to prove that they have what it takes to do something very challenging and technically involved.

No reason for doing a podcast is superior to any other. My own personal reason for starting my broadcast career was a desire to help educate the public and further their understanding of the economy and how it functions. It was my hope that once armed with this information, that people would be able to make important financial decisions using a better or improved lens. The economy and the world changed after the 2008-2009 economic collapse and this birthed new and cautious attitudes.

Traditional Keynesian Economics was creating misperceptions, poor financial decisions and potentially bad behavior. Knowledge is the key to helping people improve their lives and those of their families. (Without getting too much into the substance of my show, which isn't relevant to this point, Keynsianism is an economic theory based upon the belief that central bank monetary actions and government fiscal stimulus can help solve numerous recessions and depressions quickly and efficiently, without resorting to the free market.)

I wasn't out on a charitable mission. I wanted to eventually reap financial rewards in the form of a high income derived from profitable sponsor relationships. However, money was not my first order of business. Rather, I was looking to build a substantial audience that would share my goals.

At the time I started Financial Survival Network (FSN), I had recently sold my law firm partnership interest and was living off an income stream from prior deals. Over time, I knew that I would become more dependent upon the show's income. I have always treated it as a business. I hired an assistant/producer to handle guest bookings, perform audio editing, posting of shows and other tasks. I could have done all these things myself, however, I wanted to concentrate on improving my radio/podcasting skills. In business I feel that it's important to do what you do best and for me that's recording audio segments and analyzing news and events. I planned to keep on improving my skills and eventually be rewarded for these efforts.

It took three years before the show broke even. In the fourth year it became profitable and now it's becoming very profitable. All of this could have happened much sooner but for the precious metals bear market that began a few months after I started in 2011 and finally ended (I hope) in late 2015. My initial business model was to simply offer sponsorships to resource companies, gold and silver producers in particular. Others were doing it at the time and making substantial incomes. Unfortunately, the market had other plans for me.

Gold and silver had been the best performing asset class from 1999 to 2011. Gold had increased from $287 per ounce to over $1900 per ounce during that time. Silver went from $4 to nearly $50 per ounce. The companies in this sector were swimming in money and had loads to spend on sponsorships. But all good things must come to an end. Today gold is around $1300 an ounce and silver is close to $19. The impact upon these companies was dramatic and the sponsorship opportunities rapidly went down the drain.

It was time to broaden the appeal of the show. I started talking about health, politics, education, and virtually any other contemporary issue. I would have knowledgeable guests on to discuss these topics. Entrepreneurism, cultural and societal trends, also took center stage. No issue was off the table. I love business and feel that through my experience as a serial entrepreneur I can help people in their own endeavors. Self-improvement, by improving your internal state, or through additional training and self-investment, became a popular show topic.

In short, I would interview just about anybody about anything, as long as they were not completely stark-raving mad, well even a few of them if they were entertaining, as long as they had something to contribute. In the course of doing thousands of interviews, I only barred a few guests from future show appearances. One gentleman believed that his ex-wife and daughter rejected him because they were possessed by the devil. The other person was a poorly educated southern gentleman who genuinely believed that capital gains should be treated the same as earned income to help flatten out the income inequality curve. He may have had a good point, but he had no facts and no theory to back it up with. Pretty much his argument was, "I feel that eliminating the between capital gains preferential rate will make the system fairer."

Just Because You Feel Something Doesn't Make It True!

Always remember this, your opinion is just your opinion. In today's ultra-polarized world, all too many of us mistake opinion, our own and others, for fact. This is a major problem that is causing grave divisions within our society. As a podcaster and former attorney, I believe it is my duty to specifically state when something is a matter of opinion or fact. It's not that difficult to distinguish the two. Facts are things that are beyond reproach. They are easily provable. There are 24 hours in a day, 365 days in a year, the earth is round, etc. Opinion, Bush is the worst president of all time, Obama is the worst president of all time, etc.

Theory versus hypothesis: Here's where it gets very hard to differentiate. According to Webster's Dictionary a theory is "a coherent group of tested general propositions, commonly regarded as correct, that can be used as principles of explanation and prediction for a class of phenomena." On the other hand a hypothesis is "a proposition, or set of propositions, set forth as an explanation for the occurrence of some specified group of phenomena, either asserted merely as a provisional conjecture to guide investigation **(working hypothesis)** or accepted as highly probable in the light of established facts."

It is unfortunate that most people cannot tell the difference between the two. Theories are taken as correct until proven otherwise. Hypotheses are not trusted until so proven. Most of the Internet has devolved into unproven speculation, which makes it particularly subject to manipulation and propaganda. For my show I always aspire to tell the truth and I hope you will as well. So keep these concepts in mind. They are important and will help set your show apart, no matter what the subject.

Types of Podcasters/Business Models

What type of podcaster are you going to be? There are several types that you need to know about so you can determine your own type and what you need to be successful.

1) **Guru Income Stream:** Your podcast promotes services and products that you are selling or marketing. You might already have a business or be in the process of starting one. Your podcast will help establish your credibility and make you a guru in your field. It's simply a part of your branding strategy that also increases your business's sales. Cliff Ravenscraft became the Podcast Answer Man along similar lines. He started his podcast to promote his course, Podcasting A to Z, of which I am a proud alumni. In addition, he started a podcast equipment sales business that was netting him an excellent profit. He then started offering one on one podcasting consulting, which also became quite profitable. He's still at it, creating additional shows and income streams. You'll also see established companies like the Motley Fool, WSJ and others using this model.

2) **The Spokesman Model**: This type of podcaster starts out with a passion and then finds some company to underwrite it. They become the effective brand ambassador and get paid for doing it. It's a nice gig if you can find a company willing to foot the bill. It can be extremely profitable both to the podcaster and the sponsor. However, in the interest of transparency, these relationships always need to be disclosed. Some podcasters will even get several sponsors to join

27

together in a single show, thus furthering the income potential and the effectiveness of the show.

3) **Ad Supported Model:** This is the model I chose and it is by far the most difficult to successfully execute. Like a traditional media enterprise, you seek out multiple advertisers and sponsors. This is how radio, TV and newspaper advertising works. They create their content and attract an audience. They then seek out businesses to advertise to their audience. In addition to creating compelling content and shows, you must constantly search for new sponsors. It's a rule of media, eventually your audience gets burned out on a sponsor and the ads become ineffective. Even the best sponsors will likely find it in their best interest to stop the sponsorship; this should be expected at some point. Since inception, FSN has had over 20 different sponsors for various periods of time. Audible.com, a division of Amazon that is the largest seller of audiobooks on the planet is also a major podcast advertiser. They sponsored my show and it started with a bang. However, after six months we had reached saturation and they pulled back. The effectiveness of their message diminished over time and they moved on. So you have to be ready to move on to another sponsor as well.

4) **Listener Supported:** In this business model, the host sells subscriptions to all or part of their recording library. Sometimes the most recent segments will be free, or there will be complimentary content in an effort to sell you a subscription. If you're producing compelling, unique and somewhat proprietary content this can work well. Unless you're already a celebrity, you'll want to build a large enough audience and then attempt to

convert them. Another form of listener supported programming is relying upon voluntary contributions from your audience. You'll often see a button for Patreon, which is a contribution platform for media hosts. They'll offer a number of freebies depending upon the size of your contribution. The key is to get your audience to commit to monthly contributions that are simply auto-charged to a credit card so the process becomes unconscious. I know of one person who gets around $2500 per month using Patreon. You can scroll through their creator system and see how much each creator is bringing in per month. You can still do everything above and just use it as another income stream.

Multiple Income Streams

The secret of financial success in blogging, having a website or podcasting is **multiple income streams**. Pat Flynn of SmartPassiveIncome.com figured this out a long time ago. You've probably heard this term many times in the past, but what does it really mean? Let's explore it in a little more depth to help you fully comprehend the power and importance of what it can do for you.

If you're working a job right now and earning $5000 per month, the income you're receiving from that employment is one income stream. If you own a house that you're renting out for $1000 per month that's another income stream. If you're a freelancer, writing articles for blogs earning another $500 per month that's yet another income stream. You've got three income streams bringing in a total of $6500 per month. Not too shabby. You're becoming a master of multiple income streams.

Wealthy individuals have many income streams, most of them being passive. The Internet has leveled the playing field and allowed the average person to get in on the game. If you leverage your podcast/website/mailing list/YouTube channel properly, you will become a master of multiple income streams. It's not that difficult. Start with Google Adwords. They don't pay much, but every time someone lands on your site and clicks one of their links, you get paid. The golden age of Adwords has almost certainly passed, but money can still be made this way. I had a joint venture with Stefan, my webmaster, and for many years he cleared over $1000 per month on Adwords alone. But the revenue has steadily diminished and we've worked out another arrangement.

Next, if you host your show on Blog Talk Radio and participate in revenue sharing, they will serve up ads during your episodes. They will put up a pre-roll and a post-roll and you can choose to have mid-roll ads inserted. At present they send me a monthly Paypal deposit for $2000 or more depending upon the season.

Then of course there are the affiliate links. You can become an Amazon affiliate, Commission Junction and a zillion others. Will you get rich off affiliates? Probably not. However, Jordan Goodman of MoneyAnswers.com makes an exceptionally good living by selecting key financial affiliates that pay very high commissions.

Making money off of affiliates requires that you either have a very loyal following who will take your ads as the gospel and act accordingly or that you have a very large following so that the law of large numbers will assure that they are making a good number of purchases from your affiliates. Affiliates only pay you based upon sales so it costs them nothing to stay with you.

The beauty of this strategy is that it also costs you absolutely nothing to implement, so that you have everything to gain and absolutely nothing to lose. But you must be patient when you start out. It takes time to build an audience (although it's a lot faster using Viral Podcasting than any other alternative) and to start generating income in this manner.

Personal sponsorship sales are another way to earn substantial income and monetize your show. I've had numerous such relationships since starting out. I've had several precious metals dealers, audible books, emergency preparedness food sellers, gourmet coffee dealers and many others. Some come from networking and others come from smiling and dialing. It all depends. A recent sponsor is Liberty Health Share. They are a healthcare cost sharing ministry and are exempt from Obamacare. I found them at a Freedom Fest, a Libertarian convention in Las Vegas and switched my own healthcare coverage over to them. They have gotten hundreds of members from my show, many of whom would have otherwise not been covered and subject to IRS penalties..

You need to think out of the box when it comes to sponsors. Keep in mind that your best sponsor may have nothing to do with the industry or topic of your show. Every business is a potential sponsor. You must distinguish between national sponsors and local sponsors. If your podcast is national or international in scope, local businesses generally won't be an appropriate target. However, even if your show is local in scope, your audience could be exactly what a national or international marketer is looking for. However, it may be cumbersome for them to deal directly with you and hundreds of other podcasters and blogs. Instead, they'll refer you to their ad agency or rep, but that's okay, we've done a number of such deals.

The number of potential income streams you can realize from your podcast/website/newsletter/YouTube channel is only limited by your imagination. You can bundle website banners, links, 30 second spots, live endorsements, newsletter articles and on an on. How you charge for these campaigns is dependent upon your audience, its demographics, the financial resources of your potential sponsorship pool and how fast they will earn a return. If the sponsor is selling a high-ticket item and one sale will pay for several years of your sponsorship, then you'll have a very easy sell. If the ticket price is small and they will need many sales to pay your ad charges, it will be a harder sale. Every sponsor's needs are different. Keep this in mind and approach each with the attitude of how you can best further their business, thereby furthering your own.

For the beginning podcaster, coming up with a cookie cutter approach is usually a mistake. You'll want to come up with a basic proposal that contains three options, low cost, medium cost and high cost. Then your potential client has options and will most often choose the middle ground, which is what you want. However, always express flexibility, you can and will custom design a package that will suit the sponsor's needs, no matter what.

The next point is a big one. Always under promise and over deliver. Always give the client more than they paid for. After all, what is the actual cost of giving the sponsor five more 30-second spots on five shows that would have carried no advertising at all? You guessed it, **zero**. Be generous, especially in the beginning. But don't be a sucker. Don't allow yourself to be used. It's one thing to give away free stuff in the expectation of getting valuable business, but don't give your time away when there's little chance of cultivating a long term business relationship. It's just not worth it. When you're starting out it's tempting to fall into this trap, after all you've got nothing happening anyway so what do you have to lose? The answer is your dignity. To get strung along in the hopes of future business that will never materialize will make you feel weak and bad about yourself. Don't sacrifice your integrity in the hopes of maybe getting business.

What Are Your Goals?

Pick up any book on business you'll inevitably find a section on goals. We live in a goal driven society. We're going to discuss them in a different light. Goals in and of themselves are completely meaningless. If you say you want to have 10,000 downloads per show by December, so what! Goals only have meaning within the context of your *why*. When most people go about setting goals, it quickly devolves into writing down a wish list. There's nothing wrong with wish lists. You should have something to strive for.

I firmly subscribe to the saying, "A man's reach should be greater than his grasp." The unhappiest people in the world are those who've accomplished all their goals and haven't come up with new goals to strive for. You've probably encountered people who have sold their businesses or recently retired. They go through an adjustment phase that can be extremely traumatic and difficult. Sometimes they slip into chemical dependencies or clinical depression and require professional help.

The point here isn't to scare you into making goals. Rather, goals cannot stand in isolation. They should not be made in a vacuum. Goals need to be part of a plan. If your goal is to attain 10,000 downloads per episode to enable you to sign up three new show sponsors, that's a meaningful goal that produces something you can see and use… money.

Business Plan
Everyone starting a podcast should have a plan, preferably a business plan. I'm not going to create an entire course on the proper way to prepare an effective business plan. That's been done a thousand times before. However, you will find an outline

and link at the end of this book and I will highlight the important areas of business planning in this chapter that are pertinent to podcasting and the other web-based infotainment mediums. If you're an experienced entrepreneur then feel free to skip over this section. If you are not, please read it closely. As a serial entrepreneur, one thing that I have seen consistently is that most business people do not prepare an effective business plan. And as the man said, "When you fail to plan, you're planning to fail."

Understand, by business plan, I'm not referring to a document intended to raise money from outside investors or the detailed documents used to secure loans or business investors. That's an entirely different subject, which this book has no desire to broach. The business plan I'm talking about here is simply a brief document that is a road map on how you're going to carry out your business. First what type of business entity will you create, sole proprietorship, "S" Corporation, "C" Corporation or partnership. Then It deals with how much money you will be investing, where that money will be spent, how you will promote your podcast and key operational aspects. How will you continue to grow listeners and profits while keeping your costs low? Will you be renting office space? Will you have employees and or contractors? Will you be purchasing equipment and software? What about training? Will you need other businesses to design logos or graphics? Will you sell merchandise? All these things should be addressed in your plan. In addition, how long are you going to stay in podcasting if you aren't cash flow positive? This is a very important point that should be considered up front. What is a reasonable length of time you are willing to put in the work to see your goals met?

For myself, I always claimed that failure wasn't an option. But I know that I was really kidding myself. For three years my show lost money. I was paying a producer for 30 hours of work per week, plus all the soft costs that go along with running a show. At some point, I would have had to throw in the towel if the show had not succeeded, or at least switched it to a part time endeavor. Admittedly, it was a decision I didn't want to face and fortunately I never had to.

But your situation may be different. You probably haven't given up your day job to do this. Your resources may be scarce and you need to keep your expenses down to an absolute minimum. Now do you see why your podcasting business plan is so important? Maybe you can only afford to invest $500 per month. You had better start writing that plan today, before you record your first episode. Failure to do so could result in failure. Once you have an idea what your costs will be, you'll then be able to come up with a monetization strategy that will hopefully pay all your costs and leave you with a profit. Always aim to make a profit. In your first year this might be extremely difficult, bordering on impossible. You won't have a track record to demonstrate your worth to potential advertisers and sponsors, so it might be challenging to bring them on board. However, sharing with them a well thought out business plan can sometimes be enough to get them to give you money. When they see that you've thought your podcast out thoroughly, they might be easier to persuade. This is something you'll find out once you've started.

Another thing you should include in your business plan is an audience/download projection. This will take into account how many shows you intend to produce per week/month and how many downloads per show you will be shooting for. This is something I initially did not do, and I regret it. This is a part of useful goal setting that we discussed above. In the absence of actual results, you'll be sharing these metrics with potential advertisers/sponsors. Just spreadsheet them out building in a monthly growth factor that you believe is attainable and realistic.

Remember that this plan is not going to work exactly as it's envisioned. As Mike Tyson says, "Everyone has a plan 'til they get punched in the mouth." If it does work out, it will probably be the first such time in history. You can't possibly know what's going to happen and what the future will foretell. All we're trying to do here is set you in the proper direction, establish realistic workable goals and give you a good starting place. One other thing, once you've completed your business plan, show it to others you respect. It could be your accountant, successful business friends, other podcasters, your spouse, etc. Get some feedback and re-evaluate. It's important that you get as much valid input from others as is possible. It will make your plan more effective, realistic and reliable.

After you've been up and running for three to six months, then it's wise to go back to your plan and see how things have actually worked out. You'll be surprised. Things you were absolutely certain about may have turned out much differently than expected. Other things that you believed had a very slim chance of happening will have actually happened. Armed with your recent experience, use this opportunity to update your business plan. Revisit it every few months and update it accordingly. This allows you to stay on top of the business side of things and also shows future investors or advertisers that you are always looking forward to growth and increased profits.

Show Formats And Scheduling

As you know, there are a number of different show formats you can choose from when planning your show. Besides entertainment based shows that dramatically tell stories or provide other content, there's several other types of talk-based podcasts, 1) guest driven/interview based programs; or 2) Monologue centered where the host speaks about a subject or subjects on each segment; or 3) co-hosted or multiple hosted shows. Drama based fiction shows harken back to the golden age of radio, such as the Lone Ranger or Burns and Allen. The show *Serial* has become a major hit in that genre. This is one of the beauties of podcasting, it has brought back many types of radio that were popular before the television age came and killed them off. Podcasting is by far the greatest thing to come along for the spoken arts since Tesla/Marconi discovered the radio wave! You are truly fortunate because you can do a combination of any of the above or perhaps something entirely new and innovative and succeed beyond your wildest dreams.

Scheduling is very important. Create a release schedule for your podcast and stick to it. We don't recommend a show frequency of anything less than weekly. The reason is quite simple, bi-weekly and monthly shows have never worked on television or radio. The reason is simple, if you're not on every week; people tend to forget about you. It's very hard to remember something that only occurs monthly or every other week. As humans we just aren't programmed that way. Weekly shows have been proven to work best. They should be released the same time and day every week. Your audience will come to expect this consistency of you and will be disappointed if you don't adhere to your schedule. If you do a daily show, or multiple episodes per day, you had better stick to that as well. Anything more than daily, the timing of the release won't be as important. Also keep in mind; if you're doing 10-20 segments per week as I often do, many of your listeners aren't going to find time to listen to every episode. Therefore, they will pick and choose the episodes they like best or find most appealing. This leads to a cannibalizing of your episodes, where you only have so much audience to spread around. Therefore, you must arrive at an optimal number of segments where you will maximize your downloads per episode while putting out enough shows to keep your listeners coming back for more.

In the case of FSN, we have found the sweet spot to be 10-12 shows/episodes per week. We could probably go down to 8, but our hardcore listeners actually check out every show. You'll have to experiment if you take this path. My reason for doing so many episodes was articulated in my business plan. Very few of my competitors were doing daily shows, let alone multiple daily releases. Therefore, I decided I was going to bring a maniacal New Yorker's perspective to the space and outwork everyone. When I was doing 27 shows per week, I was only competing against myself. Magically, as I decreased the number of shows, the number of downloads per show went up dramatically. However, I don't regret the decision as I got much needed practice by doing all those extra shows. The audience and my colleagues were impressed by the amount of content I released. Perhaps some of it wasn't that great, but the experience was well worth the effort.

How Many Listeners Is Enough?

Audience size is an issue of major concern. How big an audience do you want to or can you attract? That would depend upon your business model and your target. Your audience could be billionaires who own large private aircraft; an audience of just a few hundred people, or you could have an audience comprised of millions of unemployed/unemployable millennials. Which do you think is more valuable?

Cliff Ravenscraft has always said you build an audience one person at a time. This is true on one level but not true on another. Yes, each person decides to become an audience member on their own, hence one person at a time. But, you want a lot of people deciding to join your audience one at a time. Preferably, hundreds, thousands, tens of thousands or even hundreds of thousands of people joining your audience, one at a time. Your goal is to build a massive audience, unless your audience is going to be a small niche, i.e. billionaires, of which there are precious few and I'm not sure how many of them listen to podcasts.

Obviously your distribution strategy must be designed to reach the maximum number of people. You can start gradually and build up, finding out what works along the way. Link sharing, writing articles, newsletter blasts, guest hosting and appearing as a guest are all things that build an audience over time.

When I started, I believed that achieving an audience of 1 million downloads per month would make me a media force to be reckoned with. Now we're extremely close and I'm thinking that 10 million downloads per month is going to bring in a large income and allow me to have a network of 15-20 shows. However, I'm going to need more employees (Send resumes).

So all the parts are interconnected and all of your operations have to work together or you will wind up with a mess and a lot of aggravation or even failure. Go back and look at your *why* and this will help you focus your efforts and clarify your plans.

Don't Forget The Mailing List!

Everything you do should be geared to creating and growing your email address list. There are many ways to make money on the Internet, but building a substantial mailing list is still the most surefire way to profits. It may seem old fashioned, but it is highly effective. Therefore, you must have an opt-in box on multiple locations on your homepage and other pages. Use aWeber.com or MailChimp or any number of the thousands web based email list managers. I would advise you to stick with the majors because there are many email list applications with WordPress plugins. If there's an application you want to use and it isn't compatible with your email manager, you'll have go through extra steps to integrate it and it still may not be compatible. Then you will be faced with the choice of having to switch email managers in order to use that application, which will be a major pain.

Use OptinMonster! OptinMonster is one of the most amazing plugins that I have ever seen. It enables you to create custom light boxes that will pop-up when a visitor is about to exit your site. Many times you enter a site only to be hit with an opt-in light box. This is extremely annoying and presumptive. Who are they to demand your email address so quickly? OptinMonster tracks a visitors mouse movements and won't appear until the visitor starts reaching for the "X." Then it can also be set-up to make a custom offer or offers. There's so much to it, I can't even begin to describe what it can do here. Your mailing list outreach efforts will be on steroids.

Newsletters

Back in 1998, I was practicing commercial law in New York State. I only did work for other attorneys. I purchased an email list of 67,000 NY attorneys. I started the first attorney newsletter in the state. I did 1-2 articles per issue and sent it out monthly. There weren't any list managers like aWeber back then, or if there were I didn't know about them. Sending them out was a tedious process. But it was remarkably effective. Every time I sent one out, I got at least 3-4 cases. In no time at all, the firm was thriving. If only I enjoyed the practice of law the way I do podcasting, I'd still be doing it today.

Now, there are probably millions of freebie newsletters disseminated daily. Despite the volume, many are still highly effective. It's a matter of how good your subject line is and how interesting the articles are. List managers services actually track open rates and you should be able to achieve a 20 percent open rate on your mailings. That means that 20 percent of the recipients will open the email. What they do then is anybody's guess. For a podcaster, they are a godsend. They remind your listeners of your existence, extend your channels of communication and further establish your expertise and authority. I know some people will listen to one of my podcasts just once, opt-in to the list and then forget all about me, until they receive that newsletter. Then the relationship is rekindled. They click a link to listen to a show and then get hooked on the show all over again. Many people rely on reminders today, we do it for bills and subscriptions and even for things like getting a license renewed etc. Why not for a podcast? YOUR podcast.

What should you include in your newsletter? That's really a matter of choice. If you're a good writer and have the time, then write your own articles. Include other's articles, or excerpts, but remember there are copyright laws so incorporate fair use source material. When you want to use another writer's article, send an email asking the writer if you can reprint their article or part of it and always provide a link to the original article. This is always a nice gesture and keeps things above board. Most writers love the exposure, just make sure they know what you intend to do. Include links to articles and other content on your website. Put in a number of links to recent or hit podcasts, people will listen to them, and some will even share with their friends.

You can also hire quality authors from sites like TextBroker.com, Upwork.com, Freelancer.com, WritersAccess.com and many others. The cost can be quite low and there are thousands of high quality writers vying for the opportunity to be published. Think about joint ventures with better-known publishers. Every day I get requests to publish other people's works. Usually, I don't take them up on their offers because we've already more than enough content. But if I were starting out today, I wouldn't hesitate to accept them. Another trend I've seen recently is companies offering to pay me $50 and up to post their articles on my site. Again, I turn all of them down because it's not worth the effort. However, if the quality is high and you're willing to disclose that the article is sponsored content, it could be a good revenue raising opportunity.

Sell ads on your newsletter or bundle them with sponsorship opportunities. There's money to be made here. These links work and bring in revenue to your sponsors and advertisers, often more so than just banners on your site or live reads on your podcast. It's yet another advertising opportunity. Don't miss it!

Marketing Strategy

Podcasting, like life, is all about strategy. Strategy is not the same as planning. You create a plan to realize your goals. Your strategy is composed of the techniques and methods used to make your plans happen. Creating a strategy is the most important part of making your podcast a success. How successful your podcast eventually becomes is directly dependent upon how successfully you execute the strategies in your marketing plan.

Marketing your podcast is not like marketing any other product or service you've ever been involved with. It deals with distribution, branding and getting your name out there. Of course there are hundreds of books dedicated to marketing as well as many courses and tools available. But you have to find what works for you and your plan has to be something you can and will stick to and modify as you grow to meet your changing needs. We'll go over several effective means for podcasters to get their shows to go viral, but this is an ongoing process that needs a major portion of your attention and a good portion of your time.

Building Your Audience
The FSN Way

I will give you several techniques that we used to build our listenership from scratch. Remember, I started in the same position as you. No listeners! I was posting the show on iTunes and got a whopping 20 downloads per show. It was quite discouraging to say the least. I was under the striking delusion that—If I built it, they would come. There was one problem with this theory; it didn't work! If you haven't discovered this already, you soon will. If you don't currently have an audience for your website or blog, you're starting from zero. Now, I will admit that the quality of my initial shows was quite poor, rather amateurish. Frankly, if I came across the show while searching iTunes I would have passed on it by like everyone else was doing. I hadn't yet found my inner voice. I wasn't yet a professional. I was still learning what you're reading now. There's just no substitute for experience.

Choose Your Guests Wisely
As a newbie podcaster it may be challenging to get high quality guests on your show. However, keep in mind that bloggers and other people with websites are faced with the continual challenge of coming up with original quality content that keeps viewers returning to their sites. This is a difficult challenge for even the most motivated blogger. It's hard to keep pumping out new articles, no matter how great and prolific a writer you may be. My formula, and feel free to use it yourself, was to do a great interview that showed them at their best. Many of these people, before I came around, were rarely interviewed. With my terrestrial radio calling card in hand, they usually jumped at the opportunity. A number of them became very popular guests on

numerous other shows as a result of their appearances on FSN. Talk about win-win.

To prep, I would review their latest articles, take a few notes and go for it. Usually, the product was better than they expected and they would post it on their site. Not a unique strategy, but a highly effective one. And it worked both ways, their audience became mine, and mine became theirs. Do enough of these interviews and pretty soon the download numbers start to add up.

Then I started to use Alexa ratings to find more popular websites and invite their proprietors on. It stands to reason that the more popular the site, the more popular the resulting interview. This usually held true, but not always. Other sites would often pick up these interviews up and you can guess what happened next, my interviews started going Viral. This happened recently with three interviews I did. Danielle Park, Andrew Hoffman and Greg Mannarino. See the results below. My most popular interviews ever!

Date	Listens	Title
8/17/16	108,513	Danielle Park—Subprime Auto Loans The Next Crisis? #3214
8/17/16	105,075	Andrew Hoffman—Deutschebank's Moment Of Truth Coming Soon #3213
8/18/16	114,861	Gregory Mannarino—Central Bank Madness Can Only Lead One Place #3216

When I began in Austrian Economics and alternative finance, I was a veritable unknown. However, I was very knowledgeable about these topics. I had been studying them my entire life, but I didn't have an advanced degree or have the depth of knowledge that so many of my guests possessed. But that wasn't required when it came to asking good questions or to carry on an interesting conversation. I could usually hold my own with all but the most advanced students of the subject, and even then that was great radio!

You don't have to be a world-class expert on your subject to do a great interview. (See interview section below) But the less you know, the more preparation you will need to do. It's just like being an attorney. The only difference between the good lawyers and the great lawyers is preparation. And there's the old saw about when you start out practicing law, you lose cases you should win. Later in your career it's the opposite, you win cases you should lose. Don't forget; during an interview it's always okay to admit your intellectual limitations. It makes you more human, humble and approachable.

Going for the more popular widely known guest isn't always the best strategy. I've worked with people who I knew hadn't yet reached their peak popularity, but who I believed were rising stars. Adam Clarey, a/k/a Captain Capitalism is one shining example. When I first stumbled upon his work, he was a somewhat obscure blogger working out of Minnesota. Now he's written several books and recently had a column go viral and receive 15 million page views! His site is as busy as mine. We kind of grew together. Always have your eye on emerging talent that you can latch onto and get a lift from.

Scoring The Big Interview

Periodically, you'll stumble upon the really big interview or as we call it "The Get." These can provide a steroidal advance for your show, or they may do nothing. Your big guest may be completely overexposed. If you do land that big one, go over and above with the show prep. Look for the unique perspective. If they've written a book, then take the time out to read it or at least do a serious skim. They will greatly appreciate it, because during their book promo tour they will encounter very few people who've actually taken the time out to do so. If you really want to impress, refer to a specific quote or chapter, they'll then know they're dealing with a serious professional.

Roundtables

Roundtables with several guests are a way to score loads of extra downloads. When you've got two or more popular guests discussing a topic, there's a multiplier effect. However, they can be difficult to control especially when discussing polarizing topics. If you're using Skype, try to use video and audio together. That way you can signal each guest visually when it's their turn. Audio calls make it difficult and guests can wind up talking over each other. You need to set ground rules at the beginning of the call and you'll need to ask questions and address guests specifically. When it works, it can be magical. I remember having a roundtable about Bitcoin, the digital crypto currency, with two experts. They were very passionate and quite knowledgeable. They let each other speak and it worked out quite well and the resulting stellar broadcast was very well received.

Become An Author

No matter what your area of expertise, no matter how much you've earned and how highly regarded you may be in your industry, if you haven't written a book, you are missing out. But wait, this is a book about podcasting, why should you care about books? It's called authoritative marketing. If you're selling a service or a product or are just looking to be a source of advice and knowledge, writing a book will help get you there. There's just something about having a book with your name on it, a published author; that is the ultimate credibility builder.

This is the fourth book I've written. None of them were picked up by major publishers. Rather, I did what used to be known as vanity publishing. Now it's called self-publishing and you can do it with out the vanity press company. If you can write some words on a page and do enough of them, you too can be an *author*. And if you're book is really good and goes viral on its own, a publisher might just pick it up, but even if they don't, you can still sell copies direct. Writing your own book could even open you up for being a guest on someone else's podcast or radio show.

My close friend Aaron Clarey has written over 10 books. He's sold thousands of them. Many of his sales have come from his own podcast as well as appearing on others like FSN. His writing style is quite irreverent, funny and entertaining. But he has a real message that he's getting across. His books have led to speaking engagements, a booming consulting business (www.AssholeConsulting.com) and many other opportunities.

Others have had similar results. John Rubino of DollarCollapse.com has written two books with James Turk

(Goldmoney.com and BitGold.com). They've sold thousands of copies and helped put John on the map. His websites get thousands of visitors per day.

How To Get It Done

There are a number of ways to inexpensively and quickly get your book published. You could hire a ghostwriter or use a private writing service such as TextBroker.com. Or go to Upwork.com and find a writer. The costs vary, but generally you can find authors for as little as $1000 for a 100 plus page book. Since your name is going on the cover, you'll want your publication to be of the highest possible quality. You need to check the author's other works and references to insure you have a competent person. You may have them write a sample chapter in exchange for a nominal payment. Once hired, you'll have to create a tight outline and monitor your writer very closely, remembering that the details of your topic need to come from you. No matter how good your writer may be, there will still be lots of grammatical errors, typos and bad sentence and paragraph structure. Your book will need to be edited.

At this point you can either self-edit or hire an editor. Again it's a matter of capabilities and cost. You can go back to Upwork.com and find an editor for virtually any price. Beware of doing it yourself. Editing can be a very tedious and boring process. If you're not good at grammar, you probably won't do a good enough job and your final product will suffer. As Clint Eastwood said, "A man's gotta know his limitations." In my case I have an independent editor do the first go round and then I ship it off to my sister. As an accomplished author in her own right, she also spent many years as a French teacher. No doubt, she's forgotten more grammar than I'll ever know.

Your book is now completed, what's next? You've got to get it published. That means you'll need an ISBN number and a bar code. They're a must if you sell on Amazon. Amazon has a platform called CreateSpace.com. It's a self-contained site for self-published authors. They take care of all that stuff. You just load your files and your cover and it's done. You can order individual copies for yourself or you can just wait until people place orders. You can also put it on the Kindle eBook platform and start selling eBooks, which now dominate the book market. There are even services that format your content to the specifications for each platform.

Become A Number One Rated Amazon Author

Being a number rated Amazon Author is a very prestigious sounding title. It means that you were the number one rated author in your category. It doesn't say for how long or how many books you sold. In fact it's a lot easier than you ever dreamed possible. We help people do it all the time. Our private coaching clients learn how to do it and become bestsellers literally overnight. If you're interested in finding out more, just drop us an email to kl@kerrylutz.com.

Rewards Of Authorship

It's important to understand that the goal of writing your book is not to sell 1 million copies. It would be great if you did and it would go a long way towards making your podcast go viral. But unless you've got some incredible story to tell and amazing writing skills, it's probably not going to happen. In reality, you'll be doing very well if you sell several hundred copies. Rather, the reason you're writing your book is to become a published author. Once you're a published author, you're now an expert in your field. This gives you untold advantages when you discuss your topic, after all—you wrote the book! And remember, if you promote yourself, it will also land you on other people's podcasts, radio shows and TV shows. It won't automatically happen, but if you undertake an aggressive effort, you can go on hundreds of shows getting your message out to the public. This will attract many listeners to your show, assuming of course that it's good, so make sure you do a can't-miss interview. That shouldn't be too hard after reading this book. And after all, it's your business.

One key to giving a compelling interview, when you're on a podcast or radio show, is to understand the nature of the beast. Many hosts are lazy. They want the interview given to them on a silver platter. Your interview request should always contain a digital copy of your book, a summary of why your book is important and a list of 10 questions that the host will be asking you. That way you'll know exactly what to expect and you won't be caught off guard. I know it sounds a bit contrived and perhaps inauthentic, but this is the way the business works.

(As an aside, I personally will never ask a guest pre-written questions. It just goes against my nature. I believe it's lazy, inauthentic and manipulative, but if I'm feeling off for a particular interview or the guest is a real dud, sometimes I will resort to the pre-programmed questions for a moment of relief.)

Robert Ian of ConquerChange.com taught me a great way to put it all of this into one easy step, when you're the writer. Incorporate those questions onto your back cover. Start with, "You should read this book if you want to know..." Then list the questions and the answers. When the host picks up a copy of your book after usually having done zero preparation for the interview, he'll have everything necessary to sound intelligent right there before his eyes. It works like a charm. But of course it requires that you send out hard copies of your book, which will add to the expense of your efforts.

There are numerous advantages to being an author. You can offer free chapters to get your viewers to opt-in to your email list. You can have book signings with your listeners. The list goes on and on and is only limited by your imagination. When done right, it will completely set you apart from your competition and put you into a special class. But make sure your book has substance. Keep it real. Be yourself. Make it count.

There are those marketing gurus that will tell you that just having a book cover with printed pages inside, regardless of the content, is enough, that very few people will read it anyway. And perhaps they are correct. My feeling is that if my name is on the cover and one person reads it and I'm not proud of the content, then I won't do it, regardless of the benefits. If you don't give your book 100 percent, what else are you going to cut corners on? Maybe your book won't become a literary classic, heck, maybe only 5-10 people will ever read it, but should that make a difference? Always do your best and then you'll have no regrets. It works for me.

Podcaster Copyright Issues

Your podcast is your property and is automatically copyrighted under the Copyright Act of 1976. No one has the right to use it without your express permission. However, they can use excerpts under the Doctrine of Fair Use. This allows authors, commentators and members of the public to use portions of your works within their own works. This facilitates the free and open exchange of ideas and helps further the public discourse. Of course there are limitations on the size of the excerpted portions of your work or others that can be appropriated. It's impossible to give an exact size other than to say that it's substantially less than the whole. If in doubt, reach out to the author or publisher and ask for permission. A "yes" is all you need.

The same applies when you are excerpting other people's podcasts, radio shows, YouTube videos and television shows. You can take portions of these works for fair use in your own work. The problem can arise when you use copyrighted songs that are not in the public domain. Some people believe that if they use just 30 seconds of a song, they'll be protected by Fair Use and have no liability. Nothing could be further from the truth. You must negotiate an agreement to obtain a license and pay royalties to the copyright owner for use of their work. Otherwise your appropriation is clearly prohibited by copyright law. Should the copyright owner start a legal action against you, you could be liable for up to $250,000 for each offense, which means every time your podcast was listened to. This is a potentially devastating legal tab that very few can afford to pay. Most importantly, the resultant judgment may not be dischargeable in bankruptcy. (Please note if you are on a radio station, they have purchased licenses to use published music on their stations as intros, outros, bumpers, etc. This will probably not extend to your podcast of that show. If in doubt consult your attorney.)

However, this situation is easily avoided. If the song you wish to use isn't very popular, and you're planning to use it in every show as a bumper, you might be able to license it for a very small royalty. Otherwise, find a song in the public domain or look for royalty-free music services that simply charge you a flat-flee when you purchase the song. Just do a Google search and you will find dozens of these services that provide both types of music.

Remember, when it comes to copyright, always err on the side of caution. One mistake could cost you not just your present fortune, but your future one as well. Some questions are best left for an attorney.

Trademarking Your Show

Trademarking your show can be an important step in protecting your intellectual property (ip). Unless you take the necessary steps to protect your show's name and logo, others may be free to copy and clone it. This point was brought home to me recently while attending a meeting of the Florida Podcaster's Association. One of the members recounted a story where a well-known podcaster ad agency, sponsoring a large podcasting show, used this podcaster's name, without his authorization.

This podcaster had legally trademarked his name. He brought this to company's attention and they worked out an agreement to fly him to the show, allowing him to participate in it. Other arrangements were also made, which he was not free to discuss.

Before you choose a name for your show and your company, you should do a basic trademark search. This can be done for free by going to the US Patent and Trademark Office. The website can be found at http://tmsearch.uspto.gov.

Assuming that your search comes up clean, you can then submit an application at a cost of $225 to $325, depending upon the type of trademark you are seeking. If things start getting complicated, by all means seeks the advice of an attorney.

Insurance

You should always carry general business insurance, even if you work out of your home. This will cover you if the deliveryman trips over your rug, your assistant gets carpal tunnel syndrome or a power surge wipes out your computer and you lose all your data. (This happened to me once, when a power surge destroyed my company's server. We were down for a week and were able to get a substantial insurance settlement) You'll also need workers' compensation insurance in most states even if you use independent contractors. Make sure you check this out with your attorney. States have been cracking down and each state has different laws and rules.

There is special insurance available for your podcast to protect you against defamation, slander and libel. The applications you must fill out are time consuming and vexatious, but if your subject matter is controversial, you should consider it. Your standard general business liability policy will not cover you for these acts in the absence of a specific rider, which most companies will not write. There are several specialty insurers that write this coverage. It costs a few hundred dollars per year. The plaintiff's burden to overcome and win is extraordinarily high in defamation actions; however, you may go broke successfully defending the case, if you have a well-heeled plaintiff who pursues the action all the way to the US Supreme Court. You could get stuck with a hefty legal bill and wind up in financial distress. It is wise to have an attorney available for such questions and legal support.

Your Website

At this point in the evolution of the internet, podcasting and personal branding, I'm sure that it's probably unnecessary to make mention of the need for you to create a website with the same name as your podcast, however I have learned too many times in life not to make any assumptions. Therefore, going back to naming your podcast, you will also be creating a website with the exact same name and a dot com suffix. This is an important component of your branding strategy. We all know that dot coms are much more in demand than any other suffix. The largest and most popular websites in the world all end in dot com. However, that does not foreclose you from using the second most popular site suffix, which would be dot net.

Your website's purpose is to help build your online brand and identity. At first, very few people will be visiting your site. It will be a repository for your podcasts; perhaps some affiliate links and your blog. Yes, you definitely should do a blog. Excerpt other people's articles, remember fair comment, don't take the entire article (without written permission) and do link back to the original article on their site. In addition, think about writing your own original articles and distributing them via your newsletter, yes you will be doing one of these also. Always look for the best sites in your related field. If it's podcasting go to Cliff Ravenscraft, passive income—Pat Flynn, for Amazon—Mike Gazzola, etc. My 8th grade Algebra teacher said it best, "If you're going to 'steal', steal from the best." You're not really stealing here, you're borrowing and you're giving credit to the originator and linking back. Not only is the creator getting credit but they're also getting traffic. Seems like a great deal to me.

You website is the history of your show and a record of other people's shows that you want to make note of. You can incorporate Facebook posts, Twitter feeds and anything else that you so desire. If you're computer savvy enough, do a Wordpress site yourself, otherwise hire someone. There's no shortage of people from around the globe who will be delighted to bid on your project on upload.com or any other number of project programming sites and you can always go to www.upwork.com. Be sure to check them out and make sure their prior work is of high quality.

Remember, websites start off slowly in the beginning. With very few visitors you'll be generating very little, if any revenue. Don't be discouraged. Keep at it. Eventually it will become a profit center and if you become very popular, it could become a major profit generator. You never know. But one thing is for certain; it will be a key element of your brand. Keep it up to date. Nothing is worse than visiting a website that's out of date, going months without new posts. It means you are out of date and probably out of business. This is very important to understand.

Always use Google Analytics or some other service that will track the number of site visitors, their origin, how long they spend on your site and other key information. This data will help you with sponsors and will also help you get the word out about your site. It's so important to start this when you start your site. It will also enable you to see how many people are visiting your site in real time at any given moment, which is very cool.

There are many ways to monetize your site such as: Google Adsense, where you allow Google to post ads to your site and you'll receive a few dollars a month for your efforts; putting your sponsors' links up and other ad networks; affiliate links which can be quite profitable if your subject matter is in the right niche, such as financial firms which pay large commissions.

Jordan Goodman's show MoneyAnswers.com makes an excellent return on this market.

It's just a matter of increasing the quantity of your content times the number of your listeners/visitors. Easier said than done. The point is that there is a definite formula for dealing with this type of monetization. The more content you have and the more people who view that content, especially your podcasts, the more you're going to make.

Blogtalkradio for podcasters is the icing on the cake in this regard. I've been using them to monetize my podcasts for over 1 year now. During that time they've been putting over $1,500 in my Paypal account each month. Some months are better than others. November and December generally bring in the highest revenue per ad placed, due to holiday advertising. At the present time we yield about $2 per thousand ads placed. You're not going to get rich from BTR until you're doing millions of downloads per month, but remember what we said about multiple income streams. Blogtalk is yet another example. A thousand here, a thousand there and pretty soon we're talking about real money. Since Andy Toh came on board, BTR's platform has been updated and it's really coming into its own as a major podcast platform.

Other podcast servers will also sell advertising for your show. Libsyn is probably the largest podcast server platform out there today. Their reliability is second to none. Their analytics are quite amazing. They require you to distribute a questionnaire and have certain minimum traffic requirements in order to consider your show for their ad campaigns. The advertising fees are higher and you'll wind up with more if you qualify.

Blubrry also has ad programs and each of their advertisers has specific criteria in judging whether your show is suitable for sponsorship. To qualify, you must subscribe to their free statistic service. That requires using a redirect url when posting your podcast link. Then a rep from Blubrry will periodically send out eBlasts with available sponsorship opportunities. Thad Corcoran is the brains behind Blubrry and is one of the thought leaders in podcasting today. He's always coming up with new and improved ways to better understand podcast traffic and analytics.

Another way to garner ad dollars is working with ad agencies. We've done this a number of times over the years. Ad agencies are hired by advertiser to place ads on various media platforms. Recently, a number have gotten into placing podcast ads. Generally they want high popularity, high download volume shows. It's worth keeping them in mind for when your podcast goes viral. Then they'll be only too happy to place ads with you. The rates are negotiable, but they will generally tell you what they are willing to pay and it's up to you to take it or leave it.

Content Is King

To paraphrase a campaign slogan from long ago, "It's the content stupid." The popularity of your podcast is all about the content. Make no mistake about it, how you present your content is an indispensable element of your success or failure, but ultimately it comes down to quality of content. As Valerie Geller always tells me, "Make it matter." To me that means don't get caught up in the trivial. Deal with important issues. That doesn't mean you have to be talking about world peace or nuclear disarmament, but rather about what's important to your audience. If you're talking about wooden boats, then the best means of storing and preserving them is something your audience might find significant. If you're discussing cars, your audience might not care about the recent drop in the value of the Canadian Dollar (although they probably would at FSN). But they might be very concerned about the ongoing pollution scandal at VW.

Your content must be relevant to your chosen audience. This concept of relevance and importance will evolve over time. However, when you're planning your podcast you have to start someplace. Start by charting your archetype listener. If you have a blog already and are already watching Google Analytics, for some insight take a look at your demographic data. (You might have to activate this feature) What are the age, sex, socioeconomic level, education, race, and geographic composition of your targeted audience? In other words, who are you trying to reach? In the case of FSN, I kind of felt that I wanted to reach people from 45 and up, entrepreneurs, professionals, retirees, males, females, higher earners, living in the US.

The actual demographics were pretty close, except that one third of the audience turned out to be non-US. That was a real shocker. Fifteen percent is Canadian, another shocker.

Look at a show like Cliff Ravenscraft's Podcast Answer Man. I thought his show and therefore his Podcasting A to Z class demographic would be predominantly male. I was totally off. Perhaps 40 percent of my class was female. Podcasting is a subject that appears to be nearly gender neutral as well as belonging to various income levels and all over the globe. I think you get the point. That's why it's important to revamp your listener model regularly, because you'll need to adjust your content to fit your listener profile.

It's important to understand that adjusting your content is not selling out. You still need to be authentic, original and yourself. It is simply an acknowledgement of who is actually listening to your show. The more you know about this hypothetical person, the better job you'll be able to do in providing this person with the information and programming that will keep them coming back for more, again and again, perhaps forever. If you have thousands of retirees listening daily, do you think they want to hear about childcare or how to pick out the right swing set? Perhaps they might if they have grandchildren, but that's a stretch.

When you've built up an adequate mailing list, send out a listener survey. Be as detailed as possible without being overly intrusive. Give your listener the option of not answering any questions they're not comfortable with. Some surveys won't allow you to go on to the next question without answering the last. At least give the option of n/a for a question they don't want to address. The information you receive may startle you. I know it did for me. You should do this regularly, at least twice per year. It's a great way to stay in touch and on top of your audience's preferences. And you'll stay ahead of the competition as almost no one else is doing this.

So what about the actual execution of your show? Do you need an actual script? If you're doing dramatic readings or reciting many facts, you probably do. If you're interviewing a guest, you should write out questions or bullet points, especially if it's a famous person or very well known individual. You might be nervous or keyed up and your script/notes will keep you on point and focused.

It's a question of personal style or comfort level. The key is to be able to read material without sounding like you're reading it. The master of this technique is Rush Limbaugh. Until I started doing it myself, I never appreciated how hard it was to not sound like you're reading. Rush figured it out a long time ago. While you're reading, try moving your body, a part of your body, your hands, and your feet. It really helps. Change words around, don't read verbatim, make the script your own. Once I figured out how he did it, it was a breeze.

Unless you are extremely knowledgeable about the subject matter or are an expert, talking without notes on a topic is very challenging. If you're an expert then you should be able to talk for hours on end about it. Otherwise, have a note on your computer or an index card with bullet points and perhaps an outline. Some people just need to write out their introductory sentence and then they're off to the races. Whatever works best for you. Generally, some type of structure is preferable and will make you sound better and more together.

Many newbie podcasters suffer from a belief that they will run out of topics to discuss. I'm here to tell you that this is a false belief and that if you have any passion whatsoever for the work you are doing, it's an impossibility. You should figure this out within the first six weeks of doing your show. If not and you actually do run out of material then you are in the wrong line of work and you should probably give it up.

Stumbles and bumbles are just part of the learning process. I cannot even listen to my earliest work; it's so littered with them. But I could not be where I am today without having gone through the process. I was about two or three months into the show when I realized that if I just paused for a moment, the words would come out a lot easier and virtually effortlessly. (Thanks again Valerie.) I became a lot less self-conscious and the words began to flow, stream of consciousness kicked in like magic. Give yourself a break and cut yourself some slack. Don't be overly self-critical in the early stages and you will almost certainly go through a similar process. Some people are able to sit down and write several thousand words without the least bit of effort and others can just sit down in front of a microphone and just start talking away like there's no tomorrow. But a determined student can learn both skills. I know because I didn't have a propensity for either, and now I've mastered both.

Not all of your work has to be original. Feel free to quote, paraphrase or refer to other people's work on any given topic. But always, always give attribution to that work. It's not just a matter of plagiarism, but rather you may have a listener and probably will, who has read that article and may know more about the topic than you do. Therefore, to avoid embarrassment, give credit where credit is due. Wouldn't you want someone who was using your work to do the same?

Encourage your listeners to write in. Give out your email address every show, at least three times. Listener responses are an invaluable source of material and will also give you an idea of where your listener's heads are. The more you know about your audience, the better job you'll do. Every day when I sit down, I want to do the best job that I possibly can. I'm writing this book to help you do the same. Often times, I actually achieve that goal, but even when I don't, I still achieve a level of satisfaction that's hard to describe. I have to really screw things up badly to have a bad day doing my show. That really means a lot. How many other jobs can you say that about?

Getting Started

Unless you've picked a topic that is unique and that no one has attacked before, the odds are that there's tons of material dealing with your subject on the Internet and elsewhere. Your work is cut out for you. Unless you're already an expert in your field, and even if you are, start researching. Read everything you can lay your hands or your keyboard on. I can't emphasize this enough. Malcolm Gladwell says that it takes 10,000 hours to become an expert in any subject. I agree with that statement, except that this applies to the first subject you're attempting to undertake. After you've become an expert the first time, the next time is much easier. I've become an "expert" in a number of fields, database management systems, various pc applications, judgment enforcement/lien priorities and various legal specialties, podcasting, child support enforcement, Florida foreclosure investing and precious metals investing. This doesn't mean I know everything about these topics or even most of the applicable body of knowledge, only that I'm in the top tier of people who are acknowledged experts in the field. In certain areas at certain times I could have been among the most knowledgeable. But staying there requires an obsessive desire to keep your knowledge base up to date. For most of these topics, I've let my expertise fall by the wayside by not staying current.

You might not need to become a world-class expert in your chosen field, but if you're extremely well versed, it can only help the quality and depth of your podcast. You'll never know everything; hopefully you'll be learning something new everyday. There are certain guests that constantly give me an education. I am always humbled when Rick Rule, Peter Schiff or Jim Rogers appear on my show. I feel like I'm getting a free education. I learn right along with my audience and I think they understand and appreciate that.

Once you're an expert, you'll never have a problem finding a topic for discussion again. In addition, if you plan to have guests, you'll know whom all the key players in the field are and you'll be keeping a list for future invitations. When they graciously accept your invitation, they'll be far less intimidating and you'll be able to intellectually keep up with them. This will further elevate you in the eyes of your audience and before you know it, you'll be a major authority too, especially if you've written that book we mentioned before.

That is exactly what I expect to have accomplished after printing of this book on Viral Podcasting. But seriously, if you look at the best podcasters, the people you listen to the most, at least for me, they generally are the people who appear to possess a high level of expertise in their field. Cliff Ravenscraft, Pat Flynn, Dan Carlin and the list goes on. There's just something very impressive and satisfying about listening to someone who has mastered their subject, someone who knows their stuff and knows that they know their stuff. You are completely capable and have the ability and intelligence to be one of those people too. It's not something that can be faked. Your listeners can sense fakeness and inauthenticity a mile away. You can't fake it until you make it. If you don't have the expertise yet, let your audience know that you're a work in progress and that you are taking the steps necessary to acquire the requisite knowledge.

Sometimes it isn't necessary to have that specific knowledge. Perhaps you're never going to be a rocket scientist, but you have the unique ability to help simplify the science and physics behind this subject and to help your audience learn and achieve a higher understanding. The beauty of this medium is that your area of expertise doesn't have to be in the subject matter of your podcast. You just need to bring a different perspective to your niche. The ability to reflect a different perspective is often all it takes to make you a hit. It's something you won't know until you get started.

What Now?

What is important is that you do get started. Which of course is always the hardest part and which cannot be taught. There's often just a human resistance to taking that first step to doing something new and different. Fears from our childhood kick in, fear of failure and many other issues can arise, not the least being questions of our own self-esteem. Creating a podcast is the ultimate in putting yourself out there. No matter how good your show is, some people just aren't going to like it and what you have to say. Some of them will be crazy, some of them might be scary, some of them might convince you that you're actually the crazy one, but I'm here to tell you that none of this matters. Believe in yourself and believe in your concept and take the risk! If you fail, and it's a very real possibility, at least you won't have any lingering regrets. If you defy the odds and you succeed, you'll find yourself in a whole new world, almost completely of your own making. Not trying is guaranteed failure, so take the chance and give it your all.

Since embarking upon this career, I've met some of the pillars of the alternative investment community. I've acquired scores of friends and colleagues across the globe. These are people that never would have known I existed, but for the fact I started podcasting. And my experience is by no means unique. People like Cliff Ravenscraft, Pat Flynn and all the other popular podcasters have had similar experiences. My life has not suddenly become perfect, hardly. But the podcasting journey has been a very satisfying one. After five years of intensely creating content, I still look forward to doing it every day. My passion is still as intense, perhaps more so, than the day I started.

Unlike other people, I wasn't blessed with the ability to create beautiful artwork, play an instrument, sing, write great novels, etc. However, I was blessed with a talent to speak into a microphone and my prior life experience gave me the knowledge necessary to connect with an audience about a wide range of topics. There are certainly people who do it far better than I, and I admire those people greatly, but as I continue down the path, that gets smaller every week. My goal has never been to be the number one podcaster in any particular field, but rather to be the best that I can possibly be, a long difficult mission that can be frustrating at times, but is ultimately the most rewarding career of my life.

Improving Your Quality

First you must understand that very few among us are born a radio/podcast star. Don't be too hard on yourself. I remember hearing the stories of David Letterman watching his shows and totally tearing into himself for every perceived blunder he made during a particular bit or routine. Now I have never been a big Letterman fan, but that had nothing to do with his talent or lack of. I just don't like him. But once you've made it to the top, it's time to give up all your insecurities and self-doubts and self-loathing. You worked at it, you've made it; you deserve to be there.

Actually the time to give all that up is when you're starting out. It will make your task so much easier. Do you think it's easier to succeed in an aura of positivity or negativity? But you must always be a realist at all times. Be positive, but if you mess up an interview or a monologue, be honest about it. Positivity is not an excuse for self-deceit. *To thine own self be true*. You'll progress much faster and your improvements will be much easier.

The flip side is that we really are our own worst critics, so again don't be too self-critical, be firm but not unreasonable. Acknowledge the errors of your ways and go on. There's nothing else you can do. You can't turn back the hands of time and get a do-over. Move on, learn the lesson and get onto the next screw-up, which is always lurking just around the corner anyway. It will help you to forget all about the last one.

The real radio stars among us today, Rush Limbaugh, Howard Stern, Sean Hannity, etc., developed their skills over a period of years. They used air checking and self-improvement plans to constantly improve the quality of their shows. From the start, it was a constant quest and a struggle over self. Each one of them had their own particular set of challenges that they needed to overcome. Obviously they were successful at learning from their mistakes and improving the quality of their shows, because whether you like them or not, you still know who they are. But so many of their peers and colleagues have not been as successful or enjoyed such longevity.

What separates them from their less successful brethren? In my own quest, and I don't put myself in their category—yet, I believe it boils down to commitment. Are you willing to do whatever it takes to reach the level necessary to achieve your dreams? Of course when you ask people this question, virtually everyone answers "yes." But the reality is much different. How many late evenings in the office, missed school activities and games, years without a vacation, sometime weeks or months without a day off. Are you willing to endure it all to realize your dream? Will you sacrifice your marriage? The love of your children?

Becoming a great podcaster/radio personality doesn't require you to do any of the above. That's because you only need to do a few hours per day of actual work and several more of show prep. But in terms of ego, you've got to be willing to give up the notion that you actually know what you're doing when starting out, and for quite sometime thereafter, because you don't have a clue.

Of course you'll have to act as if you do, otherwise who's going to listen to you? But really you don't have any concept of what you're doing. You're like that 16-year-old kid who just got her license. She has no experience on the highway of life and she's petrified every time someone blows their horn at her. After she's driven 20-30 thousand miles and experienced several near death experiences she starts to get the hang of things. She might even be approaching expert status; that is if she bothered to keep an open mind, studied and learned from her mistakes.

Radio and podcasting are no different. You need a constant feedback loop and an open mind with a goal towards never-ending self-improvement. The Japanese call this Kaizen. It is vitally important that you never stop your efforts to improve no matter how successful you may become. Like so many other areas of life, it's grow or die.

Getting A Coach

I knew I needed help. I was suffering from major self-doubts. Several years before I had gone out with a very successful DJ from New England and when I had shared my talk show host dream/ambition with her, she was quite adamant that radio was not for me. This doubt had stuck in my mind.

When I decided that I was going to give radio/podcasting a try, I needed an unbiased evaluation of my talent and abilities. So I decided to go get a radio coach. I was blessed to find Valerie Geller. As the author of the two best books ever written about becoming a successful talk show host, she was the perfect experienced professional to give me an honest critique and actionable advice. For many years, she had been program director of WABC-AM, then the most successful talk station in the country. She worked with Rush Limbaugh, Sean Hannity and mentored many talk show hosts who are now household names. She helped these people realize their potential and they're enjoying the fruits of her guidance and their own hard work today.

Luckily she was located in Manhattan, a quick drive down from Westchester County, where I was then living. I showed up for my first appointment. I told Valerie, "I just want an honest assessment, can I be great at this or should I stick to my day job." We played a few of my segments and Valerie did an aircheck. That's where you listen to a segment and critique your performance. It's invaluable and everyone should do it at least monthly, if not more.

She listened to my work and then said something that changed my life forever, "I wasn't sure at first, but after hearing you tell that story, I know you can do this, but it's going to take a lot of work!" I don't think she noticed (at least I hope not, but tears welled up in my eyes because she had validated my dream, and it needed a lot of validation). This was an honest assessment and at that moment I made the decision to give up the law, and several other businesses to devote myself fulltime to radio/podcasting. To this day, I have never regretted it and have never looked back.

Air checking can be a painful process. Even when you have a non-judgmental, gentle critic like Valerie, it's difficult at first. You have to admit that you are not doing the best job possible. Then you have to take the criticism, however constructive, and internalize it and do the work. Much of it happens at a very unconscious level, but you've got to take action and you have to not get hung up on self-criticism.

For myself, getting a coach was the logical course. I learned how to ski in my mid-20s. My wife insisted I get private lessons. I balked because they were quite expensive and I didn't think I could do it at my *advanced* age, but she insisted and eventually I got good enough to ski black diamond runs (though I was never great at it). Same thing in middle age, any skill you want to learn or master, if you get highly capable private instruction, it will cut your learning curving to a fraction of what it otherwise would have been.

This proved especially true with Valerie's mentoring. My confidence increased geometrically and so did the quality of my show. My association with Valerie has enabled me to turbo-charge my radio/podcasting career and shave years off of my learning curve and it could very well do the same for you.

My experience aside, I would encourage anyone who's considering taking up the call to retain Valerie or someone like her to do an honest assessment of your talents and your abilities. If you really don't have what it takes, better to find out now rather than later. You can always ignore the advice and continue on anyway. The world is full of successful people who were told that they absolutely couldn't do it, but it's always a good idea hear from an expert.

What's In A Name?
What's In Your Name?

Take a look at the iTunes podcast listings. You'll find thousands upon thousand of podcasts. Some of them are no doubt very good and of high quality. However, their titles leave much to be desired. My first show, Financial Survival Network is probably such a title. However, I stuck with it and rose beyond its limitations. A good title will separate you from the pack and help to catapult you to success. A bad title will condemn you to failure and prevent your show from ever becoming the success it should have been. Mediocre titles such as mine will neither help nor harm your show and that's a shamed.

Viral Podcasting, in my humble opinion, is a great title. It tells you exactly what the show is about and creates interest at the same time. It's short, pithy and authoritative as well. It's powerful! It shouts out its message. It's also hard to knock off or imitate. It's unique, it's punchy and it's me!

If you've realized one thing about naming rights, it is that they are very subjective. Everyone will have a different opinion about the name you choose for your podcast. Therefore, if you choose a name that you are really wild about, stick with it! Have the power and confidence of your beliefs. Let me just share a few guidelines about picking a name. It helps if people can get an idea of what the show is about from the title. However, if you've got an outrageous title that attracts attention in its own right, that's okay too. John Dumas, one of the most successful podcasters and podcast teachers around does *Entrepreneur On Fire*. Not the most dynamic name, but it's worked great for him. *Podcast Answer Man* by Cliff Ravenscraft has been a huge success and leaves little doubt as to what he's all about.

Hardcore History by Dan Carlin is an amazing podcast delving into various historical events with amazing detail and context. Leo Laporte does a number of *Netcasts* as he refers to them for his *TWIT* (This Week In Tech) Network.

In summary, a name can help a lot, hurt a lot, help a little, hurt a little or make no difference whatsoever. In the scheme of things, isn't it better to choose a name that will help launch your podcast into the realm of major success? You should spend a lot of time and effort on this. If you don't find that magic name, you're no worse off than you would have been anyway. But, if you hit pay dirt, it can shave off months or even years of effort in building a major audience.

One technique that my daughter Brittany taught me is to sit down with a pad and pen and simply start writing down words and names. She's a highly accomplished and successful digital marketer who's worked for a number of well known companies at the forefront of internet marketing. Every possible subject and word associated with your topic should be written down. Go total stream of consciousness. You keep this process up for as long as you can. Do it repeatedly. Make it a game. Get out a dictionary and a thesaurus. Find synonyms and write them down too. Have friends over and get them involved. Keep doing it and then put it away for a while. Go back to it and start coming up with titles. Come up with as many as you can.

Go through them again and again. Get completely sick of the process. And then do it again. And then put it aside again. For me eventually after repeating this process several times the right answer just came to me. If only I had tried this process when I was first starting out. Who knows where I would be now?

You Are A Communicator

No matter what your job or profession, you are first and foremost a communicator. To be successful, you must learn to communicate effectively. To a large degree, your ability to become an effective communicator will determine how successful in life you ultimately become. Nowhere is it more important than in podcasting, radio, TV or other public media positions. But how do you become a better communicator? Communication courses are taught in most colleges and universities, yet there really is no answer to this riddle. It requires an ability to think critically, listen effectively, formulate ideas and opinions rapidly, often with little or no preparation and then to speak them clearly, whether verbally or in written form in a manner that makes them easy to understand and absorb by the intended person or audience.

As Oscar Wilde said, "Anything worth learning can't be taught." When it comes to communicating well, I am convinced that this aphorism is particularly apt. When I attended elementary school and junior high, I had no interest in grammar or creative writing. Most people in the class could run grammatical rings around me. However, when I did write something, it was often far more interesting than my fellow students' work and always more memorable. What I lacked in knowledge of grammar, I more than made up for in my clever ability to communicate my thoughts. I still wound up with a C, after all it was an English course and my grammatical skills were lacking.

Humor is another very effective form of communication. Have you ever tried to teach someone how to be funny? It just can't be done. In media, humor can be deadly. For someone who never laughs, it can be a real stretch. Then there are those who think they're a lot funnier than they really are. What can you tell those people? For me, the ability to laugh at the world and myself is an indispensable coping tool. No matter how bad things have gotten in my life, as long as I can laugh, I will prevail. There have been times where I'm just not laughing much and I fail to see the humor in everyday life. When I fall into that pattern, it's a wake-up call that there's something major wrong and I better take a closer look at what's happening in my life.

I think I'm a funny person, or at least I have moments. I don't have the ability to do stand-up, but judging from the reactions of those around me, my ability to find and share the humor in any given situation seems to be a plus. I don't believe that for the past 59 years my family, friends and associates have placated or pacified me by chuckling at my sometimes-weak efforts at humor. I know that because there are people with whom I've often feigned amusement. My body language says I'm really not very amused and the depth of my laughter is very shallow, they eventually pick-up on it. I'm a bad actor.

As you can see, humor in the media is no laughing matter. Don't have enough of a sense of humor and you'll be viewed as a stiff. Laugh too much at everything and you'll be viewed as a dumb twit who just laughs non-stop. And don't forget, to some extent humor can be generational, situational (oh I guess you had to be there…) and confrontational. It's a tool to be used in your communication arsenal. Don't over rely upon it and be sure to admit your limitations. Otherwise you may find that you're the only one at the party laughing.

Communication also includes being a proficient writer. Prior to attending law school, I was a very mediocre writer, at least from a technical perspective. I dozed off in too many grammar classes. I couldn't see the value of them. When it came to using a comma, semicolon, quotation marks, etc., I was clueless. The one thing I had going for me was that I was a voracious reader.

My road to grammatical recovery started when I purchased a used copy of Warriner's English Grammar. This textbook was the bible for those seeking to master the dying art of sentence, paragraph and composition construction. I started from the beginning with parts of speech. It was amazing how much I didn't know. I kept plugging away at it for several months. Eventually all those arcane rules started to make some sense. Combined with the never-ending demands of legal writing, I somehow became a better than average writer. It was quite gratifying.

I'm not advising that you go back and repeat all those classes. Now we have the *Grammar Girl Podcast* and many YouTube videos that can help to greatly improve your literary skills. You need to be able to comfortably communicate your thoughts in written form to be a successful podcaster. But wait, all you want to do is talk. Well if you can afford to pay someone to write your show notes, fine then go right ahead. But eventually, if you are successful in your podcasting efforts, you will be forced to write articles for your newsletter or others. So just accept it, improve your skills and move on.

I hear people complain that they're not articulate enough to go on the radio or do a podcast. In most cases nothing could be further from the truth. What it really means is that you don't possess the confidence to engage in these activities. And since you lack confidence, if the opportunity does present itself, you will probably fail.

One of the most important skills you can learn is to speak in stream of consciousness with minimal or no notes. This is not easy to master. It took me years and there are times I still cannot do it. It requires you to attain a level of knowledge where you become unconsciously competent. That means you know your subject matter inside and out, backwards and forwards and every other way as well. Upon achieving such mastery, which I mentioned Malcolm Gladwell says will take you 10,000 hours, you will be able to expound upon your chosen topic for hours on end with absolutely no teleprompter or notes (except for an outline or bullet points) and you will be perceived as an expert.

To be a great podcaster you don't necessarily have to be an expert in any specific area. But, it certainly can't hurt. I'm reminded of the late great Johnny Carson. He was a comedic genius and could make it appear that the things he spent hours rehearsing were just coming off the top of his head. I'm not sure if he ever mastered anything else, other than perhaps interviewing techniques, but he was able to communicate with people from all walks of life, those with academic achievements far greater than his own and he appeared to always be within his league. That is an amazing accomplishment and one that every interviewing podcaster attempts to obtain.

Effective communication all comes down to experience. While no one can teach you how to communicate effectively, you certainly can improve your skills, at least as it applies to your media endeavors. Staying present, listening closely to what others have to say and developing a somewhat pleasing personality will go a long way towards that end. You don't have to be as funny as Jay Leno or Jimmy Fallon, but a little bit of humor at the right moment can do wonders. **Remember** this when you start your podcasting career.

How to Speak to Your Audience

The major key to attracting and building your audience isn't really a secret. Every successful talk show host, both on radio and the Internet, has figured it out, either unconsciously or through hard work, but mostly through prolonged conscious effort. It's about connecting. It can't be taught, rather it's learned over time. That's why successful media hosts are made not born. Humbly, I hold myself out as a prime example of this statement.

When I started out I often felt I was a bumbling incompetent with loads of potential. I was recording my shows without the benefit of a "board-op" (board operator). I was nervous, jumpy, completely devoid of self-confidence and virtually unable to complete a sentence without saying "um" or "ah" or any other number of stumbles. When I listen back to the early shows, it is truly a humbling and somewhat painful experience.

But the question is how do you speak to all these anonymous souls who may be listening to you? I will rely heavily on Valerie's Powerful Communicator Principles along with my own personal take on it. First, you've got to be yourself. The days of the blaring blasting 1970s radio guy have long since past. People, in general, and your audience, in particular, crave authenticity. In your real voice, speak to your audience members as individuals using the word "You." This is something that Valerie taught me from day one. It doesn't feel natural and it takes some getting used to. You should also instruct your guests to do the same. They won't be good at it, especially at first, but gradually they'll catch on. Never be boring! If you're bored, I can guarantee you that your audience is also. You're not fooling anyone nor can you.

Speak visually. Your listeners can't see, you. Use your voice to draw pictures for them. Describe things in vivid detail. Start doing it in your regular off-air life and it will come naturally while you're doing your show. And visualization is *sticky*; it keeps your audience engaged. Don't talk about how a car almost hit a pedestrian crossing the street. Rather tell how a bright red Ferrari was racing down the street, the engine was blaring loud enough to hurt your ears, at the last moment it saw the young girl crossing the street and hit the breaks, smoke pouring from the tires, the car screeching and sliding sideways, the girl looked up and froze, her eyes like those of a deer caught in headlights as the Ferrari skidded to a stop just inches away from tragedy. Which is more powerful?

Take risks, dare to be great! Brag about your stuff and always, make your guests look great, if they deserve it. Nothing makes a host look better than a great guest. And don't be afraid to do a cool segue to a spot or to end the show. Use words that are natural to you and of course as stated before, always be a good listener.

With Valerie's permission, I've reprinted several chapters of her book *Beyond Powerful Radio: A Communicator's Guide to the Internet Age—News, Talk, Information & Personality for Broadcasting, Podcasting, Internet, Radio* dealing with proper communication. What follows is by far the best material that has been written on the subject of creator types-Reactor/Generator, interviewing techniques and storytelling. I've done much research on these topics and there's a dearth of material available. Once you absorb and master these chapters you will be well ahead of virtually all the competition. These are among the most important parts of this book. Read them over several times and they will help to insure your success.

The following excerpt from Valerie's book deal with personality types in terms of whether you are a generator of a reactor. I'm not sure which one I am, which means I'm probably both. But you'll have to determine which one works for you and then act on it.

Beyond Powerful Radio Are You A Generator Or A Reactor?

"It's not what you say, it's what they hear." —Red Auerbach *Putting Your Personalities in Power: Are You a Generator or a Reactor? Have you ever noticed that some on-air personalities, while they may be completely professional, are somewhat boring by themselves? But the minute someone else walks into the studio, they seem to come alive and get much better. Some personalities seem more talented when they are performing live in front of an audience. Others are funnier, sharper, and more creative by themselves. It turns out that talent usually falls into one of two categories: generators or reactors. In order to coach talent effectively, it helps to identify the talent's strengths and natural abilities. Sometimes that can be achieved by clearly defining the talent's roles. Consultant Dan Vallie advises, "There must be an anchor or director, a creative chief, a producer, etc." But before you define the role, knowing the type of performers you are working with lets you guide them toward their maximum performance. The programmer is then able to design powerful radio by making the shoe fit the foot, instead of trying to do it the other way around. What Is a Generator? The natural skill of a generator means that he or she can easily work alone or as part of a team. A generative talent can easily visualize original ideas. (These ideas are not always good or usable ideas, but generators do tend to come up with a lot of them.) A generator has a strong, independent imagination. The generator comes up with a myriad of topics, undaunted by the blank page. True generators are rare. Generators can be the "life of the party." ...*

*Follow Valerie Geller's guidelines at the end of this book for creating powerful radio.

Become A Master Interviewer

Always treat a famous person as if they're not, and a person who's not, as if they were. John Travolta as Adam Lawrence in the movie **Perfect**.

If you're planning to do an interview based show, it's time to learn the art of the interview. First and foremost, you must become a good listener. While interrupting and cutting off guests may work on some television shows, it's a guaranteed loser on radio/podcasting. Being polite and deferential to your guests is essential. Intelligent guests automatically elevate you as a host. If your guest is a seasoned public speaker, which most of mine are, you're job is much easier. But not all of your guests are going to be erudite social butterflies, so you've got to become the master interviewer.

Few people are born with this skill. It takes much time, effort and practice to be proficient at it. Fortunately, in my case it came more easily. I remember the first time I tapped into my inner interviewer. In Summer 2011, I attended Freedom Fest, the largest libertarian get together in the world. I didn't have a microphone or a recorder, just my trusty iPhone and a recording app. Something grabbed a hold of me, I put it in recording mode and started going up to people, introducing myself, giving them my card identifying me as a radio show host with a New Jersey radio station. Boom instant credibility!

With the formalities out of the way, the adrenaline kicked in. I began firing off questions. As a lawyer, I had long ago developed the ability to think on my feet. They were good questions and the guests responded positively. By the third guest, I knew that I had found my calling. You're always told in school that there are no bad questions. When you're doing live interviews, this statement is wrong. There are a zillion bad questions and I asked many of them. However, don't dwell on them and lose your rhythm, keep firing away and don't let your guest have time to realize what an idiotic question you just asked her. The secret to a great interview, live or recorded, is the pace and the rhythm. If you master these elements, you'll never do a truly bad interview. Larry King understands this point perfectly. He's never read one book that his guests have written and isn't familiar with any of the subject matter they're discussing. He just keeps it going no matter what and never lets them see him sweat.

Substance is always king, but let's face it, unless you're on the frontlines in Syria or some other war zone, you're probably won't be doing breaking news or providing information that can't be found elsewhere. So what is the real purpose of your interview, it's obviously to inform at some level and to entertain. The definition of entertain is "to provide (someone) with amusement or enjoyment." Assuming your show is not dedicated to humor, your purpose is to give your audience enjoyment.

These are broad terms. Your audience can enjoy many aspects of your show, including your voice, your intro, the way you phrase questions, your unique perspective on the economy or the world or any other subject you can think of. You can provide hard information, with numbers, charts and analyses and still be entertaining. Entertainment is a far greater concept than just making someone laugh or feel good about themselves. Like it or not, every podcaster is an entertainer. It's just that some are better at it than others. The sooner you embrace you inner entertainer, the better and more popular your show will become.

Always Look For The Angle

You are in the story business, whether you're doing an interview or a monologue. The key to making it unique and memorable is to find a unique angle or perspective on the story. I learned this from Michael Connelly the famed detective story writer. He had been a crime reporter in Fort Lauderdale Florida. He showed up at a murder scene and saw a seasoned detective reviewing the evidence. He noticed the detective chewing on the arm of his eyeglasses and saw an indentation there from regularly chewing. Right then and there he knew he had his angle.

While I'm not doing crime stories, I often interview people that are receiving much media exposure. They've been through it dozens of times before. I don't want to do what everyone else is doing. I'm looking for the angle. If it's a mining executive, I want to know why he got into mining. Rick Rule, who's one of the savviest mining investors ever, comes from a long line of miners. I pulled this out of him and was told by many people it was one of the best interviews he ever did.

Always look for something different, out of the ordinary, off the beaten path. Remember my good friend Wayne Allyn Root's saying, "Facts tell, stories sell." Look beneath the surface for the real story that will enable your audience to connect, relate and want to come back for more.

Valerie Geller On Interviewing

I have included my mentor and coach's chapter, virtually non-redacted for the simple reason that there are few if any good books available on conducting a quality interview. When I asked Valerie for some books on the subject, she recommended Barbara Walters's book **How To Talk To Anybody About Anything.** Unfortunately, the book has been out of print for decades and it cost me a small fortune to obtain. Frankly, Valerie's advice on the topic is far more timely and relevant. I could have written far more myself, but I couldn't have done it better, so I'll let her words speak on the subject. Much of her advice deals with guests physically appearing in a radio studio. If your show is like mine, most of your guests will be making a virtual appearance via Skype. However, much of what Valerie suggests is still applicable, besides serving tea and pastries, the way you treat your guests and keep control is completely on point.

Conducting interviews via Skype can be technically challenging at times. We discuss these issues elsewhere in this book.

Interviews are a necessary part of the information-gathering process for both news and talk. A powerful interview can rivet the audience to their radios; a boring one can make them disappear.

Remember, your guests—whether rock stars, artists, politicians, experts, specialists in their fields, or "regular people" with stories to tell—may be nervous when they show up at your radio station. You go on the air every day and it seems routine to open the microphone and talk to thousands of people. However, this experience can be terrifying to "civilians," who may be nervous or forget what they want to say. They can become unsure of where they're heading with a point and become boring—talking endlessly, and saying nothing.

The purpose of an interview is to get the interviewee to open up and tell you things of interest. You may even get the person to reveal things he or she does not ordinarily discuss in a public forum. You want your guest to share information, to tell stories.

A good interviewer knows that in order to get the most out of any interview, the person being interviewed must feel comfortable. Ideally, he or she should forget about the microphone. They should feel heard. If you catch your guest looking at their watch, there's a problem because during a good interview, time should fly.

One of the best things you can do to start your interview off well is to introduce your guest in a compelling way that will excite your audience, and make them want to hear what the guest will have to say. Of course, this will benefit you, by keeping your listeners waiting for the interview to begin. But your guest, who may be exhausted from a long book tour, or anxious about doing a good job on your show, may actually feel inspired to be more candid, and a better storyteller, because you've portrayed them or their work as exciting and interesting.

Here's a typical promo or introduction to an interview:
> *I hope you'll join us for a very interesting show tomorrow… Our guest is Dr. John Johnson talking about a new study from the Health Institute. This new report shows a higher percentage of children are now being diagnosed with autism. Dr. Johnson is an expert who works with autistic children. His latest book is Understanding Autism. To learn all about autism and*

children, join us here on KXXX at 10:00 a.m. tomorrow for our next show.

After a Creating Powerful Radio workshop, the host who had promoted this interview the day before, changed his approach and introduced his guest this way:

> *Imagine you're on a train in Japan. You don't speak Japanese and you don't know where the train is going. People are talking to you. Handing you things, some are yelling at you. They're asking you questions. They seem angry with you, but you have no idea what they want. You are completely frustrated. If you can relate to that, you now understand what every autistic child feels. Dr. John Johnson, author of Understanding Autism is our guest in studio…*

It is up to you, as the interviewer, to present your guest so that the audience cares about what he or she will have to say. Grab their attention with powerful storytelling. You want your audience to stick with it, not tune out or start thinking about what they will be having for lunch or wondering if they'd turned on the washing machine.

You're the one who needs to keep things interesting.

Maintain Control

If the interview heads in a dull direction, grab it and steer the discussion elsewhere. For example: "I'm sure there are people listening now who fully understand the details of the photosynthesis process, but in layman's terms, could you explain why it's a bad idea to cut down the rainforests?" Your audience will appreciate it if you can keep your guests away from intricate and technical answers.

Often, you will be faced with an uncooperative interviewee, particularly in news situations. For example, politicians are notorious for not wanting to tell you anything substantive. They have their own agendas and want to use you and your airwaves to promote their ideas. Dealing with this tactic can be tricky.

is one method to get them to talk. It comes from Swedish newsman Stig-Arne Nordström. His technique is "getting it a little bit wrong."

> *Let's say you have a politician who is downplaying the significance of a proposed tax hike. You might say, "So your plan means no tax increases for anyone?" The politician will then feel frustrated and misunderstood. People in his profession can't stand that. He might come back with something like, "No, no, no, my plan would mean a uniform tax increase for almost everyone!" You've accomplished several things here. You got him to talk and explain it in a short form that is easily understood and you've landed the perfect radio interview sound statement. It is short, to the point, and cuts through the smoke and mirrors your interviewee was trying to use to hide his true agenda. Don't worry about the audience thinking that you are an idiot for "misunderstanding" your interviewee. If the interview is pre-recorded, you can cut out the "dumb" question and just air the tight, succinct answer.*

CNN's former nightly talk host Larry King is notorious for asking the "dumb question." He claims he doesn't read the books of the authors he's interviewing. He also doesn't admit too much in the way of show preparation. Larry King's key is to ask the questions members of his audience would ask as if they had the chance to sit down and interview the guest, and his audience could comfortably relate to this more casual relaxed interview style.

This is how just one individual interviewer, Larry King works, and while it has been effective for him, it should not be construed as an argument against show prep, in which I strongly believe. Each interviewer and host works differently. But the secret of conducting a great interview is the ability to elicit powerful stories, and glean new knowledge and information in an interesting way, where you also get to know the person. In most cases, the more relaxed and "at home" the subject feels, the better it goes. The closer an interview can be to a "real" conversation, the better it works.

Here is another, somewhat controversial, trick for pre-recorded interviews. If a guest is nervous and the answers are too formal, stilted, long, and boring, try this: Wrap up your interview. Leave the recorder running (hopefully your guest won't notice). Then say, "Just to make sure I've got this right, could we go over it one more time?" The guest, now relaxed because the interview is "over," will often tell you, in a very conversational way, what the key points were. You can then "notice" that you left the recorder running and ask permission to use that interview, instead of the first, formal session. I don't believe this is an unethical technique. After all, your guest knew that he or she was talking to you for a broadcast interview, and this audio is often much better.
Interview subjects are frequently grateful and will thank you for making them "sound so good."

The Art of the Interview: Powerful Listening
National Public Radio's Susan Stamberg got it right the skill and art of the job is to gauge the method needed to get the

interviewee to open up and talk. That "sense of approach" is a skill you develop by listening. the glorious expositions."

Stamberg, like all good interviewers, understands that, in an interview, the "star" is the topic or the guest, not the host. It helps if you, as the host, can sublimate your ego somewhat and focus completely on what your guest is trying to say. Listening is the key.

The interview will go much better if the topic is something you care about, as opposed to something you think will be of interest to your audience. Remember, "interested is interesting." If you are bored by the topic, odds are your audience will be, too. Listeners can tell the difference between affected and genuine curiosity.

Like a fisherman going for the catch, it is sometimes necessary to use a variety of baits and lures for different types of interviews. Your opening questions will depend on the circumstances. Sometimes it pays to be tough. Other times, kindness, empathy, or humor serves you best. There is no one right approach to getting a great interview. Part of the skill and art of the job is to gauge the method needed to get the interviewee to open up and talk. That "sense of approach" is a skill you develop by listening.

Uh, Uh, Uh ... Nervous Guests?
Some stations actually hand out or e-mail a list of helpful hints for guests to read before going on the air. If you would like to try this, here are some points to include.

Tips for Interviewees
Please be available and flexible. If the interview time has to be changed, be gracious. The station may call you in an

emergency, if another guest has canceled, or if the station is in need of your expertise right now. Be willing to appear. The host and station will appreciate and remember you.

If you want to make sure you get a copy of the show, have someone record it for you off the air.

If you're an author, PLEASE don't repeat the name of your new book or your website over and over. Listeners will get annoyed. Your job is to be so fascinating that the listeners stay until the end of the interview because they want to hear the host repeat the title of your book. We will put your information on our station website if you give it to us in advance.

Forget there is a larger audience. You will be much more effective if you speak to the host one-on-one, instead of addressing all those listeners "out there." The audience listens one at a time.

Try to relax. Be yourself. Radio is personal and intimate. Listeners like to be spoken to that way.

Watch your language. This is not a living room and certain expressions could slip out if you aren't careful!

Keep to the point. If you don't have anything interesting to say, ask the host for another question.

Turn off your mobile phone.

Do you understand the process? You should feel in control as much as possible. Ask how to use the cough button, just in case.

Can you stop anytime? Is this being recorded, or is it live, direct, and "anything goes"? (If the interview is live but via remote, either phone, satellite studio or via SKYPE, what is the plan if anything goes wrong?)

Don't be rigid. As in normal conversation, the interview may take a turn that has nothing to do with your agenda. Be a good guest. The discussion may lead to even better things than you were originally prepared to talk about. A skilled interviewer does not stick to a script.

Listen to the questions and answer them. If the host seems unprepared or unfamiliar with your topic, don't express anger or frustration. The audience is probably in the same boat. Just speak to the host as you would to a friendly, but uninformed, stranger you meet at a cocktail party or in the next seat on an airplane. If you can genuinely interest the host in your topic, you will also interest the audience, and will have a very good chance of being asked back.

Thoughts for Hosts and Interviewers

Forget the long hello. Keep the introduction and greeting short and to the point. *(Emphasis added mine)*

Listening is the key to successful interviews. Don't stick to a list. Often the best next question will come from the answer to the last one.

Try not to ask "yes" or "no" questions. Ask the "how" or "why" questions. Ask how people feel, and have them explain things.

If you didn't get enough of an answer, don't be afraid to ask again. This is especially important in recorded interviews when you are looking for that perfect sound bite.

Curiosity counts. If you are genuinely curious about the topic, the interview will work.

Ask "dumb" questions. Do not be embarrassed if you don't know all the answers; the audience probably doesn't either. That's why you are doing the interview.

Get to the point. Don't clutter up the interview with lots of chitchat. The audience cares about how what is being said affects their lives.

Control the interview. Steer the subject in a better direction if the interview starts to get boring. Don't let slick-talking, verbally skilled guests get around you and not answer questions. Ask your questions again, and again until you get answers, then move on.

Focus on solutions, not just problems. Even if your guests have some pie-in-the-sky solutions or can offer nothing more than a phone number to call, that's better than ending an interview on some hopeless, downward note.

Respect responses. Everyone is entitled to an opinion. If he or she is an idiot, that will come through loud and clear all by itself.

End your interviews cleanly. Do a short goodbye. You don't need to recap points made during the interview. Trust that listeners got what was discussed and move on.

On Listening

Because listening is such a part of creating powerful radio, it's worth looking at separately. Years ago, at UCLA, a friend gave me a book called On Listening by psychologist Carl Faber. When I read the following passage, I was stunned. On Listening expressed what I felt in my heart about radio— about connecting and communicating.

On rough days, I still go back and read that book again. It always helps. Creating powerful communication means powerful listening.

Dr. Carl Faber taught courses on relationships, myths, men, and women. His early UCLA lectures were broadcast on Pacifica Radio in Los Angeles.

The following is an excerpt from Faber's book.

From Carl Faber, On Listening

Most people have never really been listened to. They live in a lonely silence— no one knowing what they feel, how they live or what they have done. They are prisoners of the eyes of others, of the stereotyped, limited, superficial and often distorted ways that others see them.

There are no words to adequately describe what it is to be free with another person. It is most often a sensing that someone will let us be all of what we are at that moment. We can talk about whatever we wish, express in any way whatever feelings are in our hearts. We can take as much time as we need. We can sit, stand, pace, yell, cry, pound the floor, dance or weep for joy. Whatever and however we are at the moment is accepted and respected….

This experience of freedom and communion helps us to feel that someone is for us. And it is this deep sensing of someone, somewhere, being for us that breaks into the silent loneliness of our lives and encourages us in the struggle to be human. It helps us to break the tyranny of the stranger's' eyes and to give to our lives all that we are capable of giving. Because listening can bring about such powerful healing, it is one of the most beautiful gifts that people can give and receive.

*Follow Valerie Geller's guidelines at the end of this book for creating powerful radio.

You Are A Great Storyteller

While we are all communicators, the key to succeeding in radio/podcasting is to become a master storyteller. This is something I've been trying to improve upon since the beginning. When someone is telling me about a company and starts reciting the latest results and how sales are up 10 percent and profits have increased 15 percent… I quickly find my eyes start to glaze over. But if the same person tells me, "The Company was languishing and then they brought on a new head of marketing who really shook the place up. He upped the budget, brought in a new sales manager and sales jumped 10 percent the first month!" That's a story. Whenever I interview a guest I look for the real story whenever possible. That's what my listeners and everyone else wants to hear. It's just so much more interesting and compelling.

Unfortunately sometimes I forget this valuable rule and slip back into fact based interviewing. Maybe my show doesn't get boring, at least I hope not, but I know in my heart that I am not doing my best work. At times like this, I will re-read Valerie's chapter *Becoming A Powerful Storyteller.*

If you communicate for a living, you work in the "story business." The purpose of storytelling is to entice the listener— to make the audience want to find out what happens next. It's not all that different from childhood fairytales: "Once upon a time, in a far off land, there was a princess and a monster. Then one day…"

Human beings love stories. We learn through them from the time we are children, and continue the tradition as adults. Most people find it very hard to resist a good story! If well told, they make us laugh, entertain, teach us about life, and, importantly, remind us of our humanity. Long before the printed word, every culture on Earth passed down its vital information, its ethics and morals, through storytelling, myths, and parables. Best-selling books, movies, television, and live entertainment are all based on great stories, and great storytelling.

Storytelling is one of the key points in the proven Creating Powerful Radio/ Creating Powerful Communicator's process: focus, engage, opinion/ position, and storytelling. There are those who are naturally powerful storytellers, and the art of powerful storytelling is a talent. Any topic in the hands of a truly talented master storyteller can come alive and captivate an audience. But the craft of storytelling is a skill that can be taught— no matter what your level or talent, anyone can become a better storyteller.

The pace is accelerating. Because nearly everyone has access to media and technology, it is your well-honed ability to tell stories within the limits of your medium that will allow you to get an audience, and to keep that audience's attention. In an over-communicated world where media is democratized and mobile and everyone can be a broadcaster, producer, publisher, director, actor, and storyteller: in a time when anyone from virtually anywhere can create and send pictures, words, moving images, and audio to anywhere else, and to anyone else— one person or billions, good storytellers will rule.

The audience for all that communication is overwhelmed. They have choices—what to read, view, listen to, comment on, interact with, and pass on to others. Whether it's a 140-character tweet, a thirty-second commercial, a sales presentation, or a full video production, if it is not a good story, it won't get attention.

The Creating Powerful Radio workshop mantra is: "There are no boring stories, only boring storytellers." Whether you work as a broadcaster (or communicator of any kind), your job likely involves powerful storytelling.

Storytelling trainer and consultant Jeffrey Hedquist says, "Everyone—parents, teachers, managers, journalists, salespeople, advertising and marketing executives, and entertainers—all use stories. We either do it haphazardly, or with skill and effectiveness. You can use this inherent, powerful tribal communication skill to your advantage to influence, motivate, educate, sell or entertain your audience."

The basics of storytelling are covered in the chapters in the News section of this book, including: Who, What, Where, When, Why, and How. Beginning, middle, and ending. But it's the way you tell the story, using your own personality and tailoring it to your audience; that will make you a powerful storyteller.

Audiences connect to and respond to stories that reflect the basic themes of human nature: good and evil, right and wrong, humor, love stories, the ridiculous (life is absurd), or how an individual triumphed over the odds ("David and Goliath" or "revenge" stories). Rags-to-riches or riches-to-rags. Stories that show character and are hopeful, and teach, inspire, or move people, all work.

Tommy Kramer's Six Steps to Great Storytelling
Broadcast consultant and talent coach Tommy Kramer teaches storytelling. Kramer says,

It looks easy, and everybody talks about telling stories on the air, but only a small percentage of people on the air know how to be compelling when they open the microphone.

But the good news is that you don't have to be a born storyteller, this is a skill that can be learned. At its core, a story is simply a premise or situation that leads to some sort of resolution. What makes the average person a poor storyteller is that there is no resolution, no real "ending." It just slowly grinds down to a halt, or abruptly stops.

Most "real people" (including guests and callers to your show) can't tell stories; they have to sort of be tricked into it. For a better result: Don't solicit stories on the air. Instead, just say something compelling enough to elicit an opinion or an emotional reaction in the course of the conversation. It's your job to wheedle the story out of them.

Otherwise, you fall into the trap of having a lot of people who think their stories are interesting roll onto the air like a hand grenade rolling into the room with the pin pulled. It's not a question of whether or not it'll go off; it's a question of how many people it'll kill.

Here are the six steps Tommy Kramer uses to teach better storytelling:

1. Start with the ending. This may go against the grain of what you've been taught before, but as you prep something, start with the ending, then work back from there. A mystery writer starts with knowing who did the crime. Then he simply writes the story that leads to that being revealed. "Beginning–Middle–End" is the standard description of how a story unfolds, but in the Prep process, it should be "Ending–Beginning–Middle," because unless you know where you're going, you're going to be more likely to wander all over the place trying to find the "off" ramp.

Remember that the ending needs to be something that we haven't already heard. Be careful about verbiage repeating. Many so-called stories on the radio start and end the same way, so there's no real "destination" to our journey. It's like we got in the car, drove around the block, and ended up right back at our own front door. Plus, when the end of a story is something that you've already said, it takes away the element of surprise—something that way too many radio stations have lost, ignored, or never learned in the first place.

The beginning comes next in the prep process, because without a compelling opening thought, no one's ever going to stick around for the ending. The middle part is about editing. You can take one step away from the "main road," but then come back. Again, it's like driving. One detour, then you get back on the highway—everything's fine. But take two detours in a row, and you feel lost. On the air, two "side roads" in a row means that the listener gets lost.

2. Put yourself last. Don't start by talking about yourself. Either [1] start with the subject, or [2] start by referencing the listener. "I watched American Idol last night" is just you talking about you. But "If you missed American Idol last night" draws me in. Since you pulled up a chair for me, now you're free to relate your story, give your opinion, etc. Or, "Watching American Idol is like watching people run for class president in high school," puts the subject "on the table." From there, with that "touchstone" established, you have license to give me your "take" on what happened.

*3. **Never be typical**. Say what only you would say about the subject. If someone else would say it, automatically reject it.*

*4. **Use real language**. Use the language that actual human beings use in everyday conversations. When you get "presentational" instead of conversational, you've lost me. Don't "announce" anything. Just talk to me, like a real person—like you would by the grill if we were having a backyard barbecue.*

*5. **Don't read to me**. If you must quote something, say that you're quoting it, do it, then immediately return to just talking to me. (And make that quote a short one.) Radio is full of people reading a magazine or newspaper or website article to the listener. Just tell it to me, in your own words.*

*6. **Find another "camera angle"**. This is the best thing you'll ever learn, which is why I saved it for last. When a great film director walks around, watching the actors rehearse, he's constantly thinking, "Who do I show in this shot? Where am I going to put the camera?" A George Lucas or Steven Spielberg draws up "story boards" that are, simply, illustrations of what the camera angle for each scene will be.*

Here's how the "camera angle" thing works:

Picture the Tournament of Roses Parade. Most people in radio (and especially in television) describe things from the judges' booth, watching the floats go by. "This float is the one the Tournament of Roses Queen rides. It's eighty feet long, made of over a million roses and chrysanthemum blossoms, and took ninety-four workers over two hundred hours to make." This is both typical and boring.

But what if you describe it from the Tournament of Roses Queen's perspective? She's ON the float, thinking "I've been waving to the crowd and smiling for two miles. My face muscles are screaming, and man is my arm tired—and we've still got eight more miles to go!"

Or you can describe it from the perspective of the marching band, walking in front of the float. From that "camera angle," it's probably something like, "What's she griping about? All she has to do is sit there and wave! But I have to WALK eight more miles—and lug this tuba!"

Each of those vantage points gives you a completely different view of the same event. The better and more adept you become at seeing different "camera angles," the more interesting and engaging you'll be. Just mentally put yourself in someone else's shoes, and describe how it looks and feels from there. "Camera angles" are the hidden secret to great storytelling.

There's at least one major way in which storytelling to a radio, TV, podcast or Internet audience differs from the kind of storytelling you might do around a dinner table: At the dinner table, it is considered very rude to leave if you are bored. But if you have not given your audience a reason to stay and hear it all, they won't feel obligated to listen for long.

So, it's important to put a few essential things up front. If you are telling a story outside of breaking news, it's necessary to immediately engage and captivate your listener. The trick is to get your audience to want to hear the rest of the story, and feel they need to know how it will end. In news there's a joke: "Don't bury your lead." As with anything you put on the air, ask: "Why should someone want to listen to this?" Give the reason *someone should listen to your story before you do anything else.*

If you've ever wondered whether you're really alone in the dressing room when you try on clothes, you'll want to know about the security guard who's going to jail today …

How do you find the reason? Before any story goes to air, take it apart, look at the facts and try to see it from all angles. Who are the players involved? How can you make your listeners care about them? Who will be affected by the outcome of what you have to say? Answer at least one of these questions, and put it right up front.

Looking Through the Prism
Similar to the "camera angle," one of the techniques to help people improve their storytelling is "The Prism Method."

Have you ever held a crystal prism up to the light and noticed that each time you move it, the pattern of rainbow colors dancing on the wall changes? While it's the same crystal, and the same light, and the same wall, when you move the prism, you change your perspective on the light, and you see a completely different pattern. Thinking of yourself as the prism through which the facts of your story will pass is a good way to imagine the many ways you can approach and tell the many sides to any story.
Here's an example of the "Prism Method."

Maggie, a reporter, waits in a shop to make a purchase. As she continues to stand there, Rachel, the owner of the store, is busy talking on the phone, making arrangements to close early tonight. Why? It turns out Rachel has to close at 3:00 p.m.

because she's got to get to the airport on time to pick up her twin brother, his wife and their two-year-old daughter.

As the conversation continues, the story unfolds. Maggie learns through eavesdropping that the siblings have not seen each other for forty-seven years. They were twins, born in India, then were separated, after their parents divorced. The mother brought the baby girl to England, and the father took the boy to America. They hadn't seen each other since and neither knew what had happened to the other.

One day, the woman's teenage daughter asked about her uncle and was curious about her grandfather. She went online and conducted an internet search. In less than four days, she'd located her mother's twin brother, living in the United States. Tonight was to be their big reunion at the airport.

Maggie was a reporter and this was a story. So she said, "Excuse me, but I couldn't help overhearing…" When Maggie asked if she could come along for the reunion, the woman agreed, and that's when Maggie learned the rest of their saga.

It turned out the brother had had a terrible life growing up in America. Their father, now deceased, had been an alcoholic, and had never kept a job for more than a few months at a time. He'd had four marriages. There were times when the boy was forced to live on the road with his dad, sleeping in their car. He'd gone hungry and had never finished a single school year in the same town.

Since the young man had had such an unstable upbringing, though he had steady employment, he chose not to marry until he was in his mid forties. And he'd had his first child at forty-seven. So tonight, at the airport, the brother, his wife, and small daughter were meeting his twin sister and her family for the first time.

Now, there is no right or wrong way to tell a story, but you can use the Prism Method to find the best way for you to tell it. Maggie examined all angles of this story, to find the most powerful approach for her feature.

The Prism Method—Finding the Best/ Most Powerful Approach

1. We are a global village. With the Internet, no matter how long someone's been missing, if you have the time and patience to look, with a bit of information, and a little luck (or maybe a small miracle), you can find nearly anyone.

2. Studies show that twins often feel incomplete if separated, even it if happened when they were infants. Do you ever wonder whether twins feel like two halves of one whole? If you're a twin, do you ever feel that you are "missing" your other half if you've been separated?

3. If you've never had a good parenting model, should you think twice about becoming a parent yourself? It's hard enough to be a good partner in a relationship, but if you've never seen love modeled—or watched a healthy relationship, how can you be equipped or prepared to be a good husband/ wife or partner in a relationship?

All of these are acceptable angles with which to approach this story and they all would have worked. Maggie was trying to decide which she would use as she traveled to the airport with Rachel and her daughter. But when she saw the scene unfolding before her, Maggie knew her entry point would be the little girl. Here is the opening of her story, as it aired:

Two-year-old Liza with her dazzling smile, big blue eyes and blonde curls is sitting on her aunt Rachel's lap. Liza is exactly the same age her father and her aunt were when they were separated in India, forty-seven years ago…

This example shows how by examining the same story from all the potential angles and approaches, you can find the best, most compelling way to tell it. By using the Prism Method, you are well on your way to becoming a more powerful storyteller.

Where Do Stories Come From?

It's a popular belief that everyone has at least one good story to tell. In fact, this idea was the inspiration for a radio series, where people were urged to send in their stories, and then, if selected, narrate them on the air.

Unfortunately, having a good story solves only part of the challenge. Telling the story is, well, another story. That's how one of the most difficult-to-listen-to hours ever heard on radio came to be: People with good stories, who couldn't tell them, struggling to become storytellers in front of a studio microphone, broadcasting to potentially hundreds of thousands of listeners. I'm not sure they would have felt any better to know how it worked in practice. After a few minutes of "star-of-the-day" fishing through his vocabulary for words to describe his experience of delivering a baby in a parking lot, most of the audience had gone elsewhere for entertainment. It didn't help that the announcer of the broadcast had given the whole story away in one sentence at the beginning of the program. That's why storytelling is a discrete skill. All three basics of the Creating Powerful Radio principles apply:

- *Tell the truth*

- *Make it matter*

- *Never be boring.*

To accomplish this, there are also three more skills to practice. If you learn them, storytelling gets much easier. If you can learn to speak visually, emotionally engage your listener, and use the word "you" instead of "me", "we", or "I," you will instantly become a more powerful storyteller. You don't need to hold a national contest to find good stories. They come from everywhere. Storytelling trainer and consultant Jeffrey Hedquist says, "You can get stories from your peers, clients and colleagues as well as from simple research... but by far your biggest source of stories is you. Some of the best stories, or content for your material, come from the real lives of people you know or experiences you've had, heard about or observed.

Hedquist continues,

Your life is full of relationships and everyone you know has at least one story. Make a list of everyone you've ever known. It may take a while, and it's a list you'll continually add to, but do a little bit each day. Start with your parents, grandparents, spouse(s) and all your relatives, and work your way through to more distant connections, like bosses, customers, and club members. After every name, write as many words as it takes to remind you of at least one associated story. Some names will generate many stories. Every story has power because it's real.

When you need a story, scan your list and select stories that will work for your audience. Be able to tell a long and short version of the story. Flesh out each story, amplifying the conflict and drama. This chronological method seems to work for most people.

Don't spare yourself. Think back and make a list of those emotional markers in your life. What times in your life were the most emotional, defining, powerful, or life changing? You'll know because when you mentally relive them, you'll feel them in your heart and gut. Interestingly, if the stories are told well, that's exactly where the listener will feel them. And that's where most of our decisions are made—from the emotional center.

Can you remember when you were a "know it all?" Did you ever let someone down? Step out of your comfort zone and succeed? Lose a love? Lie, cheat, or misjudge? What experiences have changed your life?

If you ask yourself these questions or similar ones, you'll unearth memories, which you can use to craft stories for your show, your advertisers, colleagues, associates or employees. Write just enough description so you can recall the story later.

When you're under the gun to do your show, write a spot, give a speech, meet with a client or train an employee, it is not the time to make this list. Start it now, and add to it. Take five minutes a day.

Now that you have a method to pry lots of stories from your subconscious, how can you turn them into effective stories?" Try focusing your stories using the following questions.

Jeffrey Hedquist's Ten Questions for Storytellers

1. Who is the story about?

Personalize the story. The most compelling stories aren't about a company, a station or an institution; they're about a person. This person is the protagonist, the hero. Your story follows the protagonist in pursuit of clearly defined goals. Ideally, make each member of your audience the protagonist, or someone your audience will identify with. Describe them well.

Give your protagonists detailed personalities. Name them [you may use fictitious names. Then you don't have to worry about hurting someone or legal repercussions, and you can make the names tell part of the story, too: "I had a crush on Miss Darling, my third grade teacher."] What do they look like? Be specific. Saying that someone has "curly golden hair with a mind of it's own," is a better description than "blonde." Next, think about quirks, blemishes, and oddities that make them unique. Include anything pertinent about their relationships.

To add visual spice, think of metaphors—what are they like? Is the person like a porcupine or a sleek Corvette convertible? Is your boss like Mr. Rogers or Tony Soprano? Think in terms of categories when you look for metaphors. If it will help them to understand the story, make sure your audience knows the relationships between characters.

2. Where are we?

Your audience wants to know. Once you tell them, they can follow the story more easily. Set the scene for your audience. Make sure they know:

Time: year, month, day, time, season, holiday…

Place: city, state, country, home, school, office, church, bedroom, attic, sidewalk…

Atmosphere: sunny, rainy, gloomy, tense, joyous, comfortable, uncomfortable…

Event: board meeting, wedding, vacation, dinner, baseball game, seminar, movie…

A longer version of the story will have more details, but even the short version should have some.

3. What's the goal?
What do your protagonists want or need to accomplish? What do they want to change? What are their dreams? Make the goal clear to your audience. Give them a reason to care about its attainment.

4. What's the obstacle?
It does not always start out that way, but the journey toward the goal can be one from safety to danger, from the known to the unknown. The obstacle is the challenge. It's what gets in the way of achieving the protagonist's goals. It is a problem, dilemma or question. It may be another person, something physical to be overcome, or something to be learned. Often it is an internal challenge. This conflict makes the story worth telling, gives it drama or makes the comedy work.

5. What's the process of overcoming the obstacle?
Your audience learns the most from how the protagonist overcomes the obstacle. It is the method that teaches the lesson. What memories did the encounter trigger? What inner demons did the protagonist face? Think minutia; think little steps. Tell the truth. The magic is in the details. Have your

characters change, or evolve during the story. This keeps it interesting.

6. Are you showing instead of telling?

Use the active voice. Telling your audience someone was overcome with sadness is not as involving as saying, "As he heard the news, his lip quivered and a single tear rolled down his cheek." Let your audience reach their own conclusions. Don't tell them how to feel. Give your audience the gift of discovery along the way.

7. Are you keeping it interesting?

Your story should intrigue and engage the audience from the beginning, and surprise them along the way to keep their attention.

8. What's the emotional connection?

You want your audience to care, to feel something from your story. We're all overloaded with too much information. Touch our emotions and you will get our attention. If we laugh, cry, get angry or sad, become frightened or shocked, get inspired or energized, we'll remember the story and the message you wanted to convey, longer.

9. What's the point?

Is there an "aha!" moment that allows your audience to discover a kernel of truth? At the conclusion, will your audience understand what the story was about? Will they have gained an insight?

10. Is there a clear call to action?

What should the listener do to get the benefits you've just told a story about? What could the listener do to apply the insight to his or her own life?

Jeffrey Hedquist's suggestions would work well for telling a short story, or writing a novel, but for most broadcasters, opportunities for telling long stories are rare. The norm is either short, or shorter. There are exceptions, of course. Public radio stations carry some popular shows where stories are told, or read, in long-form. But storytelling does not require great windows of time.

Commercials are some of the shortest forms of storytelling. You can probably recall at least one sixty-second spot that takes you two minutes to describe. Why is that? It's because writing "short" is almost always harder than writing "long." That's true for news, ads, and features. But if you can take someone on a complete journey in thirty or sixty seconds of airtime, you are truly an adept storyteller.

Turi Ryder creates in both long and short forms. She's a talk radio host and a writer for the CBS radio news network short form humor feature, "Turi Ryder's Exception to the Rule." The comedy pieces are based sometimes on news, but more often on Ryder's personal life. You'll find it on top stations across the United States.

If you ask Ryder what it takes to tell a story in sixty seconds, she'll say: A lot of time, first, I write the story without regard to length. Then, I look at it and think, "Well, most of this has to go." So I strip out every unnecessary word. I can come down to picking monosyllables over polysyllables, for timing's sake. Sometimes it makes me sad to have to hit "delete" and lose a great line. Actually, that's a lie. If I think the line or thought was really that great, I save it to use in some other, longer, form later.

You should probably keep all the original drafts of your writing, either because there may be material in there you can gather and use later for something else, or to make you appreciate how talented your editor is. The need to make every phrase count is a good way to ensure you use the most descriptive language possible.

It's also advisable to read the piece out loud a few times—for timing and for sound. Words can be funny, not only because of what they mean, but because of their actual sounds. Sometimes, I'll try on a few words for the same thing, to see which produces the desired effect. Since I'm writing something that I will voice, I try to take the opportunity to use my voice to paint part of the picture. It all has to work together. If you can believe this, there are actually numbers that sound sillier than other numbers.

Synonyms can produce wildly different effects. What's funnier: a baby shoe, or a baby bootie? An accident or a wreck? Three hundred, or two hundred and sixty-seven? And most people speak far less formally than they write. When you read your work out loud, you may be surprised at how unnatural it sounds, even if the words are yours. Sentences have to be simple. The action goes by pretty fast, and if you have lots of dependent phrases and clauses, no one will understand your point… unless your point is to sound long and convoluted.

The radio feature I'm working on may be based on a real news story, but if you're clearly creating a work of comedy, you can cover yourself with phrases like, "I imagine…" or "It seems that…" to let the audience know you're leaving the factual, and entering the fictional.

Pick the most dramatic language you can. Use your voice. You only have sixty seconds, so you have to make the listener's mind work along with yours to see what you see. By the time it's all done, you have spent two hours from start to finish on a one-minute piece. The ratio of raw milk needed to produce a pound of cheese is more efficient.

Jeffrey Hedquist suggests you examine every part of your station for places where storytelling could make a real difference. In how many areas are you using stories? Of course, these techniques apply in all the obvious places where you need content.

But Hedquist says, beyond your newscasts, morning shows, public service programming and commercials, there is need for good storytelling everywhere: sales proposals and your station's website, podcasts and promotional materials—even your engineering department's training manuals. You'll be surprised how well your staff learns emergency procedures once they've heard the story of what happened when the last chief engineer forgot to fuel up the backup generator.

Everything is storytelling and when it's done right, it's magical. That's what NPR does right. When you cut through their agenda and their politics, you're left with their stories and their storytelling and they're just so good at it.

*Follow Valerie Geller's guidelines at the end of this book for creating powerful radio.

But I Don't Have A Great Voice

Many people shun radio and podcasting because they have hang-ups over their voice quality. You might feel that your voice is too high, not powerful enough, squeaky, weak, etc. I will confess to never having any concern about my vocal qualities. I remember getting a portable reel-to-reel tape recorder for my 12th birthday. After playing around with it, I was a little bit hung-up on the sound of my voice after hearing my first recording. I couldn't believe that that was the voice that people heard when I spoke. I didn't sound anything like that to myself. But I got over it soon enough. I know that's dating myself quite a bit, but that's how we did things in the *olden* days.

After enough exposure, I just got over it. Many radio personalities don't have musical melodious voices. Howard Stern, Sean Hannity, Mark Levin, to name just a few. Whatever failings or limitations their voices may have, it hasn't held them back professionally. At one time, getting on the air required hosts' voices to have that something extra, but at one time you were required to obtain an FCC license to be a show host too. Those days are gone. Substance/content is now king. You can have an incredible voice and yet fail miserably because you have nothing to say or you're very light on content, or you just don't sound like you know what you're talking about. On the other hand, you can be incredibly successful with a weak, poor quality voice. It's all about what you have to say and how you say it. And if you're recording a show, there are some tricks you can use to actually enhance the quality of your voice. (Special thanks to Cliff Ravenscraft, the multi-band compressor and his *special sauce* and my producer Melissa!)

So you weren't born with a beautiful baritone voice like Rush Limbaugh, well get over it! Think of a good voice as icing on the cake or a cherry on the sundae. The taste can still be exceptional and if you're good enough, no one will even notice it's missing.

You can also get voice coaching to improve your voice quality. There are drills you can do and exercises you can practice to improve tonal quality that will make you the best that you can be. But don't let your perception of your voice stop you from doing something you really want to do. Just look around at all the people succeeding with lousy voices and that should provide some comfort.

Getting Great Guests

When you start your show, one of your greatest fears/concerns is getting high caliber guests to come on. How do you do it, after all you're a newbie with zero credibility and no audience? For me, that's one of the reasons why I started with terrestrial radio. I did a *pay for play* show on a 50,000-watt station in Hasbrouck Heights, NJ. It covered all of the New York City Metro area, but required an hour drive in each direction to get to the studio, a major time-waster. I did it through an organization that promised to make me a profitable radio show host in no time flat. I wasted 5 months and thousands on their program. However, the one benefit was that I actually had a show on a radio station. This allowed me my pick of guests. Instant credibility and seriousness attaches to you when you're on *real* radio that's hard to equal when you're on a podcast. As I always say, "Any *schmuck* with a microphone and a computer can do a podcast."

In addition, being on terrestrial radio means you have to follow a format and a show clock. This is extremely important as it provides discipline and forces you to keep the show moving.

Once I realized that my station had recently reformatted and had almost no audience, I bid them adieu. I found a small low wattage station in Greenwich, CT that had a very small geographical footprint. I did a weekly one-hour show, which cost me about $200 per week. Greenwich was the perfect place, because every financial guy in the world knew about this town. There are more investment bankers, hedge fund managers and other Wall Street ne'er do wells than just about any other place on the planet. When guests were invited to appear on a Greenwich radio station, they jumped at the opportunity.

What I know now is that none of this was necessary. Being on terrestrial radio did help make me a better host more quickly. But, I could have done it all on podcasting and saved a lot of money in the process. I did immensely enjoy what I was doing and the experience was irreplaceable and indispensable. It may help you to do a stint on terrestrial radio, but don't feel like it's mandatory.

Technical Aspects Of Podcasting

It's important to understand that the technology in podcasting is constantly changing. New podcast servers are always coming on line. Software used for recording and editing is always being upgraded. Custom solutions geared specifically towards podcasters are being created that will hopefully further advance the state of the art and best practices. While the hardware required for podcasting evolves gradually, change is always in the air. Therefore, it's important to keep up with these changes so you can improve your quality and production process where possible.

Equipment To Mix or Not to Mix—What Microphone Should I Get?

Purchasing equipment can be done for a few hundred dollars or a few thousand. It's your choice and your budget. You decide the level of technical proficiency you want to acquire and then how much you want to spend on it. For me, I went the $1500 route, Heil PR-40 mic, Mackie ProFX8 Mixer, Behringer Gate-Compressor-Limiter, microphone boom stand, pop filter, shock mount, special Tascam iPhone interface and backup Shure SM58 beta microphone with stand. Lots of cables, cheap $20 Sony headphones—super comfortable and that's it. For software I use Adobe Audition and Skype record for Apple. It all seems to work for me. I use Libsyn and Blogtalkradio as podcast servers. I used to use an external recorder as Cliff Ravenscraft recommends, but it became a royal pain and I just record on the computer with Audition and Skype Recorder. Always have a back up copy of any interview you're conducting. I've still managed to lose about six interviews because of computer crashes in five and half years. Not too shabby. But it's the worst feeling in the world when you've crushed that interview and then you lose it. You have to go back with your tail between your legs and meekly ask your guest for another shot at it.

That's not to say that you couldn't have a great podcast for a couple hundred dollars. **Stefan Molyneux** of Freedomainradio.com has 10's of millions of downloads using a $100 USB mic and some simple editing software. So does Jason Hartman of JasonHartman.com. But I'm a techie and a bit fanatical about my production values. This works for me! It's your money and your goals to guide you in your decision about show production investment. I'll discuss some considerations on the subject below.

There's a lot of controversy over mixers. A mixer, simply explained, takes several channels of sound coming from different sources such as microphones, Skype calls, sound effects sources, music, etc., then allows you to control volume and tone, and then combines them into one track (mono) or two tracks (stereo). Without getting into a bunch of technical issues, which I don't fully understand the physics of anyway, I wholeheartedly believe that any aspiring podcaster should acquire a mixer that has a USB input, which plugs directly into your computer. This will enable you to record Skype calls and other online calls and adjust the sound levels of the person you're speaking with as well as your own. You can record this call with a program such as Skype Recorder for the Mac and Pamela for the PC and skip the need for a mixer altogether, but I never do that. I like having full control over my recordings. To eliminate the need for a mixer, you will require a microphone that plugs into a USB port on your computer. The Audio Technica ATR 2120 is a good example and is available for around $100 on Amazon today. It's of pretty decent quality and will work just fine.

If you're going to have multiple people in your studio speaking on multiple microphones, you'll need a mixer and regular XLR format microphones that plug in. I am partial to good old made in the US of A Mackie Mixers. They are the most reliable, durable and all around best mixers available, at least in my opinion. I recommend a USB mixer that will plug right into your computer and eliminate the need for you to figure out what the hell a *mix minus* is all about. Again, there's a dozen videos on YouTube that will explain this. If you get a USB mixer, then doing Skype interviews is pretty much plug and play.

No matter what type of microphone you buy, USB or one that plugs into a mixer, always purchase a dynamic microphone. Cliff Ravenscraft taught me this in the first class of Podcasting A to Z. If you go to any audio store, such as the *Guitar Center*, they will almost always tell you to buy a condenser microphone. This is one hundred percent wrong! Condenser microphones are great for singers and music where sound range and sensitivity is essential. With a condenser microphone, you'll literally capture a pin dropping in the back of a concert hall. For podcasting you just don't need this type of sensitivity. A dynamic microphone has a more limited range and therefore it will not capture a lot of extraneous sounds that you don't want to record anyway. So always stick with a dynamic microphone.

The podcasters microphone of choice is the Heil PR-40. It's used by Cliff Ravenscraft, Leo Laporte, Adam Curry, myself and many others. It can be purchased in the mid $300 range. It is my personal favorite, being extremely proficient at capturing those rich bass tones. But it's not the only great sounding mic. The best selling dynamic mic, perhaps of all time, is the Shure SM58 with its distinctive ball shaped screen. I've owned several over the years and it's a workhorse that will never break down. They can be purchased new on Amazon for around $100 or used on eBay for much less. The updated version, the Shure SM58 beta is even better and can be purchased new for $160. It's an amazing mic that is one of my personal favorites. It's my backup mic.

Another piece of equipment that I recommend and use, especially if you're doing loads of content and can't stop hitting the keyboard and otherwise making noises that get picked up when you're recording, is a Behringer gate-compressor-limiter. It will enable you to filter out background noises such as keyboard clicks, sinks running and leaf blowers. At around $100, it's inexpensive and a pain to setup, but well worth the investment.

Microphone booms and shock mounts are also highly recommended. The boom arm will enable you to easily move your mic around your work area and keep it out of the way when you're not using it. The shock mount will stop your mic from picking up mild vibrations and light taps such as when you accidentally hit your desk.

A windscreen/pop filter is also advisable. This is a sock or a screen that goes over the mic and keeps those pesky "P's" from popping and getting picked up by your microphone.

Finally, if you're going to have several people in your studio as well as doing a telephone or Skype interview, you'll need a headphone amp/splitter to accommodate multiple headsets. Otherwise, your additional guests will have no way to hear the caller. I recently bought a Pyle 4 channel stereo headphone amplifier on eBay for around $20. It allows for up to 4 headphones to connect off of your mixer's single headphone jack and each one has an individual volume control. A useful item indeed.

As far as actual setup of your equipment goes, just go over to YouTube and search Podcast Mixer Microphone Setup and you can watch several hours of instructional videos on the proper setup of your studio. It's fairly easy and straightforward. It just takes a little time and effort to get things properly configured. It can be frustrating at times but eventually you will figure it out. It ain't rocket-surgery!

You'll need editing software. Two programs I use are Adobe Audition and Audacity. Adobe Audition is the gold standard and is quite expensive, but can be paid for on a subscription basis for around $24 per month. Audacity for the Mac or PC is free. Audition is quite a bit more powerful, but we're just editing voice recordings so much of that power will never be needed or utilized.

If you have a Mac you can also use Garage Band. That's what I started off with. There's no right or wrong way to process a file you've recorded. Just don't make your edits too obvious or your audience will wonder if you're cutting out important stuff. Some people cut out their breaths. I personally don't do it a lot, only during the first 2 minutes of a show at most. At gate compressor limiter can dramatically minimize your breathing noise.

You'll want to normalize your recording. Filter out static and taps, maybe use a touch of compressor or reverberation, use a hard limiter and some other minor effects. Don't try to make your podcasts sound too perfect. You're not a professional radio station or sound studio. If you try to sound like one, you'll probably fall short and sound somewhat fake. It's better to sound natural and real, that is part of the beauty of podcasting. Why kill it?

Below is Cliff Ravenscraft's recommended Podcast Hardware Package. With the exception of the external Roland Recorder, which as mentioned, I no longer use, but the package is a good example. Also, at this point I would only consider purchasing a USB enabled mixer for two reasons, first it's a snap to set up and second, it gets rid of the need for an external recorder while doing Skype interviews. It doesn't really cost much more and it's totally worth it.

One other extremely useful piece of equipment is the Tascam iXZ. This is an interface that will allow you to put calls from your iPhone or other smartphone directly through your mixer. At $49 it's quite inexpensive and does an incredible job. It's an amazing piece of technology that plugs right into your phone's headphone jack. That way if Skype is down or you're having trouble connecting with your guest, you can use your cellphone. Just be certain to block incoming calls so you won't be interrupted. Verizon's has an HD quality phone plan. If you and your interviewee are both have the service, the quality can be superior to Skype with fewer issues.

Podcast Equipment Package

The Podcast Equipment Package Includes:

Roland R-05 Digital Recorder
Roland Recorder Power Adapter
FREE Digital Audio Recorder training tutorial included ($39 Value)
Free Inside The Studio Tutorial Tutorial included ($100 Value)
Heil PR-40
Heil PRSM-B Shock Mount
BSW RE320POP Fine Mesh Metal Screen Pop Filter
Heil PL2T Heavy Duty Mic Boom Arm w/ C-Clamp
Mackie 1402-VLZ4 Mixer
Sony MDR-7506 Large Diaphragm Foldable Headphones
QTY 1 Standard XLR Mic Cable
QTY 1 2 RCA male plugs to 1/8" Stereo plug Cable
QTY 1 1/8" Stereo plug to 2 1/4" Mono plugs Cable
QTY 1 1/8" Stereo plug to 1/4" Mono plug Cable (not displayed)
Shipping Included! (Continental United States Only)

Skype Interviews

If you're planning to conduct interviews by Skype be prepared for the technical mishaps that you will encounter regularly. The first is setting it up. You've got to do a mix-minus, unless you've got a mixer with a USB input. There's many YouTube videos that deal with the topic.

The next challenge is the technically ignorant guest. This is the hardest problem to solve. Your guest uses a substandard headset or worse yet uses their computer's built-in microphone and built-in speakers. This setup almost guarantees awful sound quality and harsh echo. You're almost better off just using Skype and calling their cell phone or landline. It's really hard to deal with.

Skype is still a work in progress. There are dropped calls, fade-outs, spikes, garbled sounds and a host of other audio issues. It seems that Skype has more moods than... well, the most moody person you can think of. Some you can edit out and others you'll just have to live with. You can try turning off the video and see if that improves your audio, sometimes it will and sometimes it won't. You can hang up the call and try again. You can reboot Skype and reboot your computer. Eventually, you'll run out of options and you'll either have to dump the interview or live with it. I've done both.

There's a new service called Skype TX that supposedly addresses all those issues, but we'll have to see how good it really is. And as a premium service it comes at a premium cost. It also requires a $3000 piece of hardware. Is it worth the price? Question to be answered.

Intros and Outros

You should have a brief intro and outro for your show. You can pay someone to do it or go to fiverr.com and hire someone very inexpensively. My friend Darryl Tott does great British sounding intros at a very affordable price. Always put your website url and a very brief description of what your podcast is about. If you offer products or consulting services be sure to mention that as well. This is a major part of your branding effort. Your intro and outro can be set to music, it's your call. I prefer musical intros, but not everyone does. Copyright laws apply to this aspect of your show as well. Don't use *Purple Haze* or *Hey Jude* and be upset when you receive the cease and desist letter or worse. Just like you wouldn't be pleased if someone appropriated your show for their commercial benefit, don't do the same thing to an artist or other content producer. A great source of royalty free bumpers and music loops is the Garage Band Program that comes free on every Apple Computer. The loops can be used free of charge in any intro, outro or bumper without permission from Apple. They are professionally produced and many of them sound amazing. After your intro, you can have a few seconds of music too, but that's optional.

Sound Effects During the Show: The Foley

If you have a show that lends itself to live sound effects, use an iPad tablet, or other brand as a Foley. Simply plug it into your mixer and set it up and it's ready to go. There are cart apps that enable you to play any sound effect upon demand by pressing a button on the screen. They're very cool and easy to use. They'll add a level of professionalism and sophistication to your show that most podcasts won't possess.

How To Do A Commercial Or Spot

Types of commercials: There are 30 second spots, 45, 60, etc. There are also live endorsements. They're almost too clever. You'll be in the middle of your show talking about a related subject and then you segue into your client's product or service and give it a personal endorsement. Rush Limbaugh is a master at this. He'll be talking about an identity theft story and the next thing you'll know he'll be extolling the virtues of *Lifelock*. When done properly this is the most powerful radio ad in existence. I've done them for *Liberty Health Share*.

You will find that the ads you do for products you're currently using are the ads that get the best results Sometimes sponsors will give you pre-recorded ads to run on your show. Hopefully you'll be technically adroit enough to get them properly queued. It's not too technically challenging!

They may give you a script to read. Fine, again don't make it sound like you're reading. In radio that's a major no-no. Instant audience turn-off! When you do read something, as mentioned before, use lots of hand movements and gestures. It will help make it sound natural and animated. Notice musicians always move a part of their body when singing or playing an instrument. Keep rhythm. Don't do it in a singsong or a monotone. Your audience will hate you for it! Speak in an animated tone! Vary your cadence and your tonality. You shouldn't scream but you can whisper for effect.

Don't be a one take Tom either. Tom Carvel, founder of the Carvel Ice Cream Chain was famous for doing horrible commercials. He was known as "One-take Tom." No matter how bad the spot sounded, Tom did one take and he was done. Do as many takes as you need to get it right. Your sponsor is paying good money so you better get it done right or don't bother!

Podcast Host Servers

Every podcaster needs a podcast server to carry their shows and to archive them. In theory you can host them on the same server that does your website, but don't think about it. This just doesn't work. That's because podcasts are bandwidth hogs. If your podcasts get downloaded thousands of times, it will place an undue burden upon your web server (Godaddy, Hostgator, Bluehost, etc.) and they will quickly become very unhappy with you. They may issue warnings that you're exceeding your bandwidth limitations or they may just go ahead and shut down your site with no warning at all. Either way, it's not worth the risk of having your website closed out and the resulting loss of web traffic and credibility.

Therefore, to avoid this problem altogether, set up a podcast host server prior to starting your show. There are dozens of podcast server sites available to you. I personally have used 5-6 of them during my career. I currently use Libsyn.com, Blogtalkradio.com and Blubrry.com. I recommend that you stay with one of the major companies. When it comes to podcast servers, your number one concern is reliability. In my experience every server will encounter technical issues and outages at some point. You need to know that the company will rapidly address any such issue that arises. The three services listed above are extremely conscientious and responsive. They strive for 100 percent reliability and most days are successful.

The next decision you will face is choosing a service plan. Virtually every podcasting company has a free plan that allows you some minimal monthly usage at no cost. Don't bother. Go for the plan that costs around $20 per month or more. This will give you at least one show per week and some basic statistics or analytics.

Splurge on the plan that provides decent stats or what's now referred to as analytics. Blubrry and Libsyn give some really great metrics. Blogtalk is getting better by the day. They'll tell you where you're listeners are coming from, country, state and city. They'll also let you know what type of software and hardware you're listeners are utilizing, whether they're listening on smartphones or desktops. Some of the info is more significant than others. Check around and see what fits your needs the best.

Blogtalkradio.com gives two new metrics that no one else currently provides. They're fascinating and quite scary. One is a stat called **abandonment**: the percentage of people who dump your show within the first two minutes and the other is **completion**: the percentage of listeners who stay with you for 80 percent of more of the segment. These stats are great because you'll find out quickly if your intro is too long or if your segments are too long. If more than 10 percent of your audience bails on you within the first two minutes, you better take a closer look at your intro. You're losing people for no good reason. And if less than half your audience isn't staying on for most of your segments, you had better figure out where you're losing them.

Hire A Producer

When I started out, I was fortunate to have some extra money but I was unsure what direction to follow. I wanted an assistant to book interviews and to take care of all the web postings and social media. What I really needed, but didn't yet understand the concept, was a producer. I wanted someone to process all my files, clean up them up, add the intros and outros plus any ads and then post them to the numerous platforms and blogs I was using. Ideally I wanted someone to write my show notes as well. I went through several people until I better understood my needs and the proper job description. I realized that having someone handle the bookings and post-production were the most important aspects of my workflow. I could do the show notes myself, having someone else do it would take too long and wouldn't lead to satisfactory results.

After several attempts, I found Melissa who's been with me for over two years. At this point she really understands me, I know that whatever I require, she will get it done. But this comes at a price. If you don't have the funds or can't afford to expend them in this way, go back to your business plan and figure out where to get the revenue to pay for this person. I assure you that it is the best investment in your success that you can make.

I have found the alternatives to be lacking. For example, there are numerous companies that advertise solutions for editing and producing your show files. I'm extremely wary of them and the claims they make. I've found their turnaround times are iffy. For a daily show such as mine, they are not cost effective. I'm not comfortable with the idea of giving up control either. Their business model calls for having multiple clients, so how are they going to resolve conflicts and when will my work be put on the back burner? It's not something that I want to find out, just to possibly save a few dollars. It's either: do the job yourself or have an employee/contractor do it. That way you've always got accountability and your work will always come first.

Workflow

When you start podcasting, you will quickly get an education in workflow. There are a lot of moving parts to the process. First, you've got to create your content or podcast episodes. Then the resulting audio/video file must be edited and processed. Next intros/outros must be added along with any ads or spots to be inserted. Show notes, graphics and images have to be placed. Then postings to websites, blogs and social media must get done. Are you posting to YouTube? My producer Melissa and I have internalized all of this, so it's second nature by now. There are companies that offer a solution to do it all for you and are quite good and trustworthy. Some things like social media can be automated. Others can't. At least in the beginning, you need to write it all down and maybe even put it in a flow chart. Eventually it will become second nature. But just because you've got a workable workflow doesn't mean you're done. You've always got be looking to improve your workflow no matter how well it seems to be working at the present time. The better your workflow goes, the more consistent your show product will be and the more comfortable and addicted your listeners will become. It's a definite formula that has worked wonders for me over the years and it will do the same for you. It's almost guaranteed.

If you're doing a weekly podcast, be sure to release it the same time, same day every week. If you're doing a daily show, release it at the same time every day. This is so important it cannot be overemphasized! Consistency and predictability will let people know you are dependable and they can count on your podcast. I'm doing multiple shows per day and it's extremely challenging to release shows on a predetermined schedule. However, my listeners know that the show will always go on.

Control of workflow is the key to keeping your show production values consistent and high. Even at this point in the evolution of podcasting there are too many shows with low production quality. When I hear one of these, I almost always blank it out, even if the content value is high. I must ask, can't you invest a hundred bucks to do this right? If you can't be bothered to get it right, why should I listen? There are too many people doing this thing right to bother with lazy podcasters. Make the investment and aspire for high production values. In the end, it will make you shine.

Podcast Square/Artwork

In order to get your show on iTunes you must create a podcast square. If you're good with Adobe Photoshop, or other graphics programs, you can probably create one within 30 minutes. If not, you'll have to have a graphics person do one for you. The cost varies. If someone is creating your website, then simply have them make a podcast square at the same time. Most people will tell you that it should reflect the look and feel or the branding used on your website. I will take slight issue with that belief.

My theory is that at some point in time your podcast will be featured on iTunes. You want your square to stand out among the myriad of squares that appear there. You'll be competing with hundreds of shows. If you're an attractive female, by all means, use a non-sexual-feminine picture of yourself to garner attention. If you're not so blessed, like most of us, then simply use color to do the job for you. I've found that orange, yellow, gold and black accents stand out quite well. Beware of letters and graphics, since these squares show up as one inch by one inch squares on most people's monitors and tablets. They'll be even smaller on smartphone screens. That's why color is the best way to get attention. It's also why I don't worry if they are slightly out of sync with the rest of my website's branding. In the scheme of things, your square is really an insignificant part of your overall branding, but it could help get you organic subscribers from iTunes.

I'll never forget my first experience with this phenomenon. I was positioning Mike Gazzola's *Real Estate Investing That Works Podcast*. We made it to the top three investing podcasts. We had scores of reviews, we were crushing it with downloads. There was an attractive woman whose podcast stayed ahead of us for weeks. She had minimal reviews and episodes but a killer picture that showed her off to great advantage. I was ready to tell Mike to hire a model for his square, but finally after the 6th week, we were getting 3500 downloads per day and we blew past her. We kept the square with the *boring* graphic. It's proof that content always rules!

If you're at a loss of where to get your square done, go to Fiverr.com and search for Podcast Square graphics, you'll find tons of artists who'll do a great job for next to nothing. I've gotten many created for five dollars, plus an additional ten dollars for overnight service. They're perfectly fine.

Show Notes

Once you've decided to do a new podcast, you'll need to compose show notes. Show notes are a summary of your show. They can be detailed or they can simply be a one or two paragraph wrap up of the episode. It's really a question of person style. Some people like Cliff Ravenscraft or Jason Hartman do very detailed notes. They list virtually everything that happened in the show, links to guests and their websites, things that were discussed and the exact times that things happened. They believe that a potential listener will closely review these notes before deciding whether to listen or not. In addition, there's a theory that the more that's in the show notes, the more that Google will pick up, index and make searchable.

The alternative is what I do, a one or two paragraph summary describing the key takeaways or concept of the podcast. It's hard to determine which is better. However, it is essential that you provide some type of show note. There are some podcasts that have no show notes at all. Early on I tried not doing any and found that these episodes received far fewer downloads than those that had even a very brief summary. It appears that your audience just wants to know what they're getting themselves into before they start listening.

I recommend that you experiment with both approaches. If you have time do the detailed approach. If you can get someone else to do them for you, then definitely more is preferable. In my case I was doing 20-25 episodes per week and there was no way I had the time to go in depth. I'm not sure how much difference it really makes anyway; I've never been able to find anyone who can give a definitive answer. Of course the more your write, the more Google will pick up and index, but will that really help? You'll have to answer that one for yourself.

Regardless which show note strategy you choose, pay extra special attention to your title! Cal it click-bait or just good marketing, but it is the largest factor by far in whether someone or anyone listens to your podcast. Avoid overly salacious headlines; after all we're indulging in the practice of yellow journalism. However, a little impactful headline writing is more than appropriate. Remember that the highest paid employees at the New York Post, the biggest tabloid paper in the country, are the headline writers. Tabloids live and die on the strength of the *quality* of their headlines. So does your podcast episode. One technique that I sometimes use is to find trending topics on Google and Facebook. If they're relevant to my topic, I'll go out of my way to include them in the header. If you do it right, you may have an episode go viral for no other reason.

Transcribing Your Shows

Transcribing your shows is another *controversial* topic. Using offshore outsourcing, it is possible to get entire transcripts of your shows done very cost effectively. These transcripts can then be repurposed to write blog posts, white papers, combined to write your book and even a monthly or quarterly compendium of shows. Blogtalkradio even provides the service to its customers.

The cost will vary, depending upon the provider and the quality of the service. For myself, I have never really entertained the idea. It always seemed like an added cost with not a lot of benefits. Transcribing all of my episodes would have led to several thousand dollars in additional overhead per month. I guess I could have *written* 50-100 volumes by this point, but for what purpose? In addition, there's the accuracy factor. To be useful, all of these transcripts must be proofread. This is extremely time consuming and quite a bore. Of course you could hire someone to do it.

Adding the transcript to the show notes could be a plus for your SEO, but again, how much is it really worth? Could I take that $2-3000 and put it into Facebook ads or Google ads or something even better that I've experimented with and get a much higher return? Probably so. Again this is something you will have to determine on your own. You might decide that it's worth doing important shows or several per week. I've thought about that too and will probably experiment with that concept in the near future.

Search Engine Optimization

Search Engine Optimization or SEO is something that has never been a major pre-occupation of mine. For those of you who are not familiar with the concept, Google scans your site regularly using a software device known as a crawler. It indexes all of the content on your accessible pages and ranks it accordingly. It gives you plusses for things like mobile-friendly content, original content and other things that are only known to them. There are entire industries that have sprung up to assist websites in getting the highest SEO rating so that your page will rank high in organic Google searches.

I don't doubt the efficacy of SEO or these services; it's just that my techniques never focused on them. I was able to build my audience without resorting to them. I have an SEO plugin for my Wordpress site. A fair amount of my traffic comes from Google searches. My site also aggregates news content, a practice that Google frowns upon. There are services that can backlink your postings to thousands of other sites and this will raise your Google rankings. If you've got some extra capital, it's worth the effort, just remember that eventually it's the quality of your content that matters.

Cliff Ravenscraft

Cliff Ravenscraft the PodcastAnswerMan.com has been an important mentor in my podcasting career. Cliff's podcasting journey is worthy of at least a book and perhaps a made for TV movie. His career and perhaps his life looked pretty well set. He was poised to take over his stepfather's successful insurance agency. There was just one problem; he hated insurance. Through a series of events, he came to realize that he loved podcasting. He broke the news to his stepfather and soon started a podcast, providing a weekly recap of the hit TV series *Lost*. Before he knew it, he was getting 30,000 downloads per week from an international audience.

He found that he was quite proficient at getting these episodes out and started his PodcastAnswerMan.com series. This led him to equipment sales, one on one coaching, consulting and pretty soon a mini-empire. I don't mean to make it sound like he was an overnight success. Not so, it took several years. But Cliff had found his calling. He was making a substantial income all from podcasting related ventures. I discovered him through a simple Google search. I wanted to find out how to produce high quality podcast segments. Talk about a guy who dominated the organic search! I signed up for his Podcasting A to Z course. It was the best thousand bucks I ever spent. Prior to taking the course, I was recording my shows on a Blue Snowball Microphone and using Apple's Garage Band to process them. As Cliff said during the first online class, "A well produced segment won't get people to listen to you, but it will keep them coming back." Prior to taking the course, I was getting a few hundred downloads per episode and maybe 2-3 thousand per month. Before the class was even finished, I was getting 25,000 downloads per month! I was on top of the world.

I upgraded my equipment to a Heil PR-40 microphone, a microphone boom, noise shock mount and a mixer. I had a professional set up. I was editing every episode and cleaning out the buzz and static. I was almost a pro! And I developed my audience building techniques that I'm sharing with you here.

If anyone understands how to create a successful podcast, it's Cliff Ravenscraft. He now goes around the world getting paid to speak about the subject. He's a humble man and I've learned a lot about podcasting and life from him. His unselfish nature and his desire to see his students succeed has touched my life and so many others. I could not pay him back even if he would allow it. But just being able to call him a friend is a major reward in itself.

His Podcast Answer Man episodes are free and they are a must for any aspiring or established podcaster.

Distribution

How do you get your show out to the world? Believe it or not, distribution is the key to your show's success. The more creative your distribution strategy, the more viral your podcast will go. Obviously, the first thing you will do is post your completed, edited podcast to your podcast server. Then you post it to your website of the same name. That should get you your first 20 downloads. Congrats, you're now a podcaster. Now is not the time to rest on your laurels. What else can you do to make things really happen?

RSS Feeds
Virtually every distribution platform that will carry your podcast, other than your original podcast server site, will rely upon your RSS Feed, otherwise known as Really Simple Syndication. My RSS Feed for Libsyn is http://KerryLutz.libsyn.com/rss. This feed will allow any other platform or site to pick your shows automatically. Once you've established your show on Spreaker or Slacker, every time a new episode is released, it will automatically get picked up on that site. This makes distribution to these conventional outlets a snap. In addition, your WordPress website already has the ability to create RSS Feeds. It's relatively simple and easy to do and you can use that feed for iTunes and other channels.

Interested listeners also have the ability to subscribe directly to your RSS Feed. They can do it through their email program or custom newsreader program. RSS is also used to disseminate written content, although it has been losing popularity for that purpose for quite some time, because there are so many other better ways to get news. However, for the foreseeable future RSS and podcasting will be connected at the hip. Therefore, it's a good idea to provide an RSS Feed link on your site to help your listeners subscribe via this method.

The grand daddy of podcast distribution models is of course iTunes. If you're not familiar with iTunes here's a quick explanation. The iTunes program comes with all Apple computers and can be downloaded to any PC. It allows you to buy music, movies and videos from the Apple Store and to download and subscribe to any podcast that has an RSS feed listed in the store. It's been with us since podcasting began. It singlehandedly put it on the map. We all owe them a debt of gratitude because they have never monetized their podcasting platform and have made it free for all. At some point in the future don't be surprised if they say *enough is enough* and then come up with a monetization scheme. Of course they no longer have a monopoly on podcast distribution, but by some estimates roughly 35-50 percent of all shows are distributed this way. Time will tell.

There have been a lot of changes recently to the podcast section of the iTunes store. This is how it worked before and may work again. Keep checking it out. The new and noteworthy section lists 20 new podcasts for 8 weeks. There is no explanation how a podcast lands there. It probably has something to do with the number of listener reviews and the number of plays it gets through the iTunes player or downloads through iTunes. You can help influence your position using a number of strategies. The important place to be on iTunes is the *Top Audio Podcasts* section. iTunes somehow through an algorithm rates the shows, both generally and by category, i.e. health, business, comedy, etc. To be number one on all podcasts you will need a number of reviews, at least 50, and around 15,000 downloads per day through iTunes. These are not easy numbers to achieve. It's hard to game the system, but it can be done. However, it can be costly and if Apple finds out what you're doing, they will *Sandbox* you, or take your show out of the rankings altogether.

You need to get reviews. First, tell all your friends, family and business associates to download your show and review it. You can never have too many positive reviews. Apple filters by IP address so they will catch a lot of bogus reviews that Fiverr and others sell. So play it straight. Honesty is the best policy.

Even getting into the top 10 on the iTunes platform can be a major help in making your show go viral. I've had clients hit number 1 for all podcast categories. They got thousands of listeners and subscribers. This alone might be enough to make your podcast go viral, but don't count on it. iTunes alone is not a strategy for success. You've got to do much, much more if you are serious about going viral!

And iTunes is no longer the only game in town. As more and more people listen to their podcasts on their phones, the Android phone operating system is involuntarily becoming a major podcast disseminator. While the Apple iPhone makes billions of dollars yearly, the largest share of smartphone handsets in the market place is dominated by Google-Android. Google's music service will carry them as well as a number of other services known as podcatchers. These catchers pickup virtually every RSS feed from iTunes and enable Android apps to carry these shows. You should register for as many Android apps and catchers as you can. First go to Google's music play service at www.PartnerDash.Google.com. Here are several good Android apps to be aware of, BeyondPod Podcast Manager, DoggCatcher Podcast Player, Pocket Casts, and Podcast and Radio Addict. Please note there are many, many more.

iHeart radio has become active in podcasting. Presently, only the largest podcasters are getting exposure here. However, you can expect them to become more and more prominent. iHeart is the reconstituted Clear Channel Radio Corporation. They have recognized that the future of radio is on the internet and they're rapidly embracing this destiny. Hundreds of their stations are on their app, along with their most popular shows. It's obvious that they are completely committed to this vision. So pay attention to opportunities to be carried there. Libsyn now allows all of your shows to be posted on there.

Audible.com, the audio book division of Amazon is also making a play for the podcast audience. They've recently introduced a curated podcast channel with select podcasts appearing there. They intend to become a major player in this area, so this is another emerging trend that you need to be aware of.

Other Platforms
Slacker, Spreaker, Stictcher and Soundcloud are several other competing players in the field. You can easily get your podcast carried here and elsewhere, usually for free. If there's no cost, then by all means sign up. You'll get several listeners, maybe more, each time you do.

How many platforms you get your podcast onto won't make a lot of difference in the long run. Yes get your podcast on to all the free services like Slacker, Spreaker, Blubrry, etc. You'll pick up a few listeners here and there. But they are not going to be your key to success. Rather, getting your podcast on sites with the highest number of viewers is the key. And doing that is as much an art as it is a science and has been the key to my success and also why I have relatively few iTunes subscribers, unlike almost every other podcaster in existence. But more on this later.

Social Media

Virtually every person on the planet is now familiar with social media. There are scores of social media sites but by far the two most popular are Facebook and Twitter. If your show falls into either site's younger age demo, these sites will be very effective for building your audience with very little expenditure of time and money. The key to making them work is to build up your followers. This is somewhat time consuming but well worth the effort. It's something you can do yourself or hire a company to do for you. I will confess that I have not made the best use of Twitter. While all of my shows automatically get posted to Twitter, Twitter works best when you post snarky, pithy clever comments that demonstrate your brilliance.

It's just not my thing. But at some point, perhaps I will get more engaged. Facebook is much more my cup of tea. Many people, especially the stunted millennial generation gets virtually all of their news from this often-distorted source. Therefore, you should create your own page and feverishly post content. Invite everyone you know to join that page. Post comments to the page and join as many related groups as you can think of. Become very active and post your episode links all over the FB universe. It will pay major dividends, I promise you. Hire a virtual assistant to do much of this work for you. You can find virtual assistants in the Philippines and other countries for less than $100 per week. They speak excellent English and due to the time difference, they work while you sleep. You have to be very specific about the work you want them to do and what you want them to write. If handled properly, they can be a real plus in this application. In the interest of personal disclosure, I have never used a VA to do this for me, but I know many people who have.

Reddit is another social media platform that I will only briefly mention here. Articles are posted and comments are well received. It can be quite effective. Quora is similar. They both have huge followings and can be effective for your show.

A Worldwide Audience

Is your show's message national or trans-national? In what part of the globe will your audience reside? When I started FSN in June 2011, I wrongly assumed that my audience would be just like me, people born and raised the in the good old US of A. I couldn't have been more wrong. As it turned out, just two-thirds of my audience is US based. Surprisingly, 11.4 percent are from our neighbor to the north, Canada. And then comes the UK, Australia, and Germany for a total of 220 countries and foreign locales. You too may be quite surprised at the international appeal of your show. Depending upon your subject matter, you could be getting listeners from many different countries.

International is certainly the way to go. If you can format your show so that it's less US-centric and has a more global appeal, then by all means do it. We're getting to the point where there's a worldwide audience for just about any subject matter. If you obtain an audience that's a majority non-US, it could open up major opportunities that you never expected.

A word of caution: I highly recommend against creating or changing shows solely to garner audience share. First, you must be true to yourself. If internationalizing your show makes you less enthusiastic and makes the entire process less pleasurable, don't do it. You have to be yourself and love this process. Otherwise, you will fail. Only change your show or concept if it feels right to you and in keeping with your values as a business owner and podcaster. Your audience is much sharper than you could ever imagine. They know when you're bored, when you're unhappy and when you're in the zone. They can smell phoniness a continent away. So don't sacrifice your authenticity in search of audience share and downloads. It's a losing proposition and a sure fire way to fail. But as stated above, you can still target and refine your message to get the greatest listener base possible. We all do that.

Here's my audience breakdown as of recently:

United States	10,374,829
Canada	1,691,411
United Kingdom	461,883
Australia	439,083
Germany	162,106
Singapore	132,020
Netherlands	128,246
Other Regions	103,483
Sweden	97,244
New Zealand	70,449

In the beginning, I started thinking that there must be a better way and eventually I found it. Actually better ways. Viral Podcasting is a strategy. It's many things you do and many things you don't do. First some things that didn't really work.

Buying Traffic

A relatively new twist on an old method of building an audience has recently emerged and that is simply paying for traffic. Call it advertising or whatever, you set aside a budget and create campaigns aimed at getting people to your website or directly to your podcast. As of now, extremely well-heeled podcasters have been rumored to be using this technique. The most cost effective venues will be Facebook and YouTube but for different reasons. Facebook lends itself for podcast advertising because of their ability to target your demographic audience. There is no other website on earth that possesses the insight into its user-base that Facebook possesses. The cost is low. For $20 you can put together a barebones campaign. When you start investing $100 or more per day it can be extremely effective. They also have Facebook opt-in campaigns to increase the size of your mailing list. These too can be very effective. Amy Porterfield has really mastered the art of Facebook advertising. All of the major companies are using it. You just have to decide if the increase in your listenership is worth the added expense. If you're receiving CPM revenue this will be easy to determine. Otherwise the analysis will be more difficult to determine. YouTube is great because it too is so cheap. The dirty secret of advertising on this channel is that Google has way more inventory than they do customers. Therefore, you're able to purchase pre-roll ads extremely cheaply. Whether people who click through to your site will become avid listeners is another question, which you must answer for yourself. Targeting is easy, you simply pick-out channels and videos that are relevant or connected to yours. If you have a real estate podcast then look for real estate related YouTube channels to target. Doing one on finance? Look for finance channels. It all works very well and can increase your audience substantially in a very short period of time. Of course there are many other places to advertise, but that requires a lot of work and targeting. All part of your marketing plan.

Success Story 1

In 2015 I was doing well, my audience, while not growing geometrically, showed steady increases and I felt that I was on my way. I also started doing real estate on the side because the Florida market was chock full of opportunities. I had purchased a course on distressed real estate investing from Mike Gazzola. As part of the intro, he offered to take me on a property tour of Lee County Florida, an area that was devastated by the 2008-09 crash and was just starting to emerge.

I joined Mike on the tour and found that I really had a love for this business. The idea of taking properties that often needed much work and turning them into inviting places where people wanted to live and raise families, really excited me. I made an off the cuff remark to Mike that was to start me down a new path in podcasting. I said, "Mike you need to do a podcast. We'll talk real estate and foreclosures and tax deed sales and it will be a hit." He liked the idea and immediately and enthusiastically agreed. Thus was born the hit podcast, "Real Estate Investing That Works."

I became the co-host, technical guy, producer and my producer Melissa was responsible for editing and posting the episodes. The show was doing quite well; getting a couple of thousand downloads per episode when I had a brainstorm. Why not put it on the homepage of FSN? The first episode posted on the site rapidly got 20,000 plus downloads. After each new episode, I repeated the process and achieved similar results. Our most widely heard show received over 30,000 downloads! Gee, audience building is so simple. Hardly, we got lucky. To date the show is approaching the magical 1 million-download number. Mike's gotten hundreds of qualified leads and has sold many courses to dedicated podcast listeners.

Success Story 2

A friend of mine was selling an identity theft solution online. Sales were so-so and I pitched him on the idea of doing a podcast. Thus was born *The Identity Theft Warriors*, *Your First Line Defense Against Identity Theft*. The company never took off, but that didn't stop the show from succeeding. We realized tens of thousands of listens per episode. I had no idea how interested/fearful/intimidated people were by this crime that's been growing at an epidemic like speed. Again, I acted as the co-host and I interviewed Pat the expert. My producer Melissa became highly skilled in locating identity theft experts and data security specialists for the show. To date, we've done over 50 episodes with downloads in the hundreds of thousands. While the sponsorship is gone, the show lives on because I'm interested in the topic and more importantly, so is the audience.

Success Story 3

John Rubino is an author and hosts an extremely popular website DollarCollapse.com. He's been a guest on my show for years. I kept gently nudging him to start a podcast. Finally, I said it enough and he broke down and made it happen. We've been doing it for less than six months. During that time we've gotten hundreds of thousands of downloads with virtually no publicity at all. He simply posts the new show on his site, I post it on mine and he does an eBlast letting his audience about it. In some respects this is the easiest show I have ever done. John does the recording himself, it's a monologue and it's quite good. He's a natural. It's been getting picked up by other sites and it was an immediate success. The lesson here is that you can use your existing website and business model to create a successful podcast. We've gotten sponsors and it's a profitable endeavor for both of us.

Success Story 4

Jason Hartman has been an FSN sponsor, almost since the beginning. He's an extremely successful real estate investor who now helps ordinary people accumulate single-family homes for the purpose of earning monthly cash flow. He's been doing it for the past decade and has thousands of happy clients. His 10 rules of investing should be required reading in every finance class in the country. He used his podcast to attract over $12 million in revenue over the past 10 years. Many FSN listeners have gone on to become successful Hartman investors. He's one person that I never have any hesitation referring family, friends, business associates or listeners to. He approached me several months ago about expanding his audience.

Easily done, I started posting several of his shows per week on the FSN homepage. He's getting over 100,000 downloads per month, all in a very short time period.

Success Story 5

David Fischer has been selling bullion for 23 years. During that time he's become an accomplished media personality, appearing on numerous shows. He even tried his hand at podcasting. He is incredibly talented, great voice, amazing command of his subject matter, which just happens to be my favorite subject as well, or shall I say my original subject. Unfortunately, David's podcast hadn't really gotten much traction. His downloads were minimal and he had virtually no audience reach. A perfect example of what we've been discussing, a quality production with minimal outreach leading to limited success. A mutual friend introduced us and I got to work listening to a number of his episodes; from a content/technical perspective he seemed to be doing everything right.

We re-branded his podcast, *The Golden Rule with David Fischer*. We did eight shows and then released it on my site. I thought it sounded pretty darn good. The audience agreed. Much to my surprise, from the beginning David started getting calls from interested prospects. My strategy for the show was to build up David's expertise and reputation so that he would eventually become a **widely** respected expert in the field. This space is extremely crowded with hundreds of writers, podcasters, YouTubers, etc. It's not easy to break-in, but within three episodes, David is crushing it. It's partly due to my assistance, but I give the lion's share of the credit to him, because of his truly superior skill set. He just needed a little push in the right direction to make it happen.

The best part, when it came time to renew, David insisted I remain as co-host. Usually, I sign up for a three-month stint, get the client up and running and succeeding, then I happily fade away. So I was quite flattered that he requested I stay on. Hopefully one day in the near future David will go solo. He's got the talent and the ability and truth be told he really doesn't need me.

Success Story 6

Mike Gazzola, the real estate guy discussed above, called me excitedly one day. He and a partner started a new venture that was going gangbusters and they wanted to collaborate with me to start a new podcast. It seems they had mastered the art of selling on Amazon, bringing in thousands of dollars in sales every day. Now they were teaching a course and it was time to let the world know via a podcast. I always enjoyed working with Mike and jumped at the opportunity. We set the podcast up and it was off to the races. From the beginning, it exceeded our high expectations, getting tens of thousands in downloads and many thousands in sales. It has become the leading podcast on successful Amazon selling. He's been in the Top 10 of iTunes Podcasts a number of times. As I write this book, he's number 6 in iTunes Business Podcasts, right after Dave Ramsey and Tim Ferris. Pretty good company I'd say.

Success Begets More Success

As you can see from the above case histories, Viral Podcasting is like any other successful business strategy. Once you have a system in place, have your workflow and processes created, you simply repeat the process and watch the results happen and the revenue flows in. There's no mystery here. The key is to get to this point. There's lots more I could have and would have done to further boost these shows, but it wasn't necessary. Spending a few thousand more on back-linking, hiring spokesmen/influencers and a myriad of other strategies could further launch my show and my clients' shows into the stratosphere. But, I'm saving these techniques for further down the road when we've plateaued and need a shot in the arm to further increase traffic. One day, perhaps soon, I will launch a show and use every technique that I've learned over the past 5 years to propel it into super stardom from the start. It will be interesting to see how fast and how far it can go and where it will wind up. But for now, I'm sticking to accomplishing the goals as they're laid out in the plan.

What's Next?

What is important is that you do get started. Which of course is always the hardest part and which cannot be taught or forced. There's often just a human resistance to taking that first step to doing something new and different. Childhood issues arise, such as fear of failure, fear of rejection, fear of speaking to a large audience as well as questions of self-esteem. Creating a podcast is the ultimate in putting yourself out there. No matter how good your show is, some people just aren't going to like you and what you have to say. Some of them will be crazy, some of them might be scary, some of them might convince you that you're actually the crazy one, but I'm here to tell you that none of it matters. Believe in yourself, believe in your concept and take the risk. If you fail, and that is a very real possibility, at least you won't have any lingering regrets. If you defy the odds and you succeed, you'll find yourself in an entirely new world, almost completely of your own making. Isn't it worth the risk?

Conclusion

Now you know what is necessary to become a successful podcaster. The information you've received has not previously been available in just one place before. Up until now podcasters had no choice but to try different approaches and techniques on their own. In the earlier days of podcasting, when there was less competition and it was more of a novelty, it was easier to stumble around and succeed. Now as the market continues to evolve and perhaps even mature, things are no longer so simple or easy. You must have a more disciplined approach as well as a plan for success. A preferred business model and a targeted audience are now an absolute must. Trial and error is still a valid part of the experience, but can never take the place of careful planning and strategy.

But your plan is only part of your job. Becoming an effective podcaster means being an excellent communicator. Since you weren't born with these skills and probably weren't taught them either, you're must develop them on your own. This is a challenging endeavor for the most articulate among us. For those of us who haven't had careers or life experience connecting with large groups or have avoided doing so, you're in for some rough seas ahead. However, this is where your passion is essential. If you truly love this journey that you've undertaken and there's nothing else in the world you'd rather be doing, then your skills and capabilities will progress on a natural upward trajectory. The inevitable setbacks will be minor and short-lived. You'll easily prevail because you'll always have your vision set upon your ultimate goals, the obtainment of which is an absolute certainty (of this I'm sure).

Finally, you'll master the challenges of creating compelling and brilliant content that will keep your audience growing and always coming back for more. You'll be amazed at how creative you can become and the talent you'll develop for attracting people to your message. You'll discover an entirely new dimension to your being that you never knew you possessed. I've personally experienced this profound transformation and I've seen it take place in countless others. It's not painless, but it's not unpleasant either. You just need an overwhelming desire to make it happen and then take action to see that it does.

Many days, when it all comes together, the experience is otherworldly. Then there are days when it doesn't happen and it's like the golfer who's just having a bad day and can't get the ball on the green in less than five strokes. You just focus on the memories of getting it right and eventually the magic returns and you're back in the game, better than ever!

So please take the lessons of this book, the ones you find most useful and go forth and help bring the art of podcasting to levels not yet seen or experienced. For there are truly no limits to this emerging medium, except those we impose upon ourselves.

Consulting

For those interested in advancing your own podcast and making it go **Viral**, I accept several clients per year on an application basis. I work with people I know I can help and who are involved in areas that I find personally interesting. For select clients I will help co-host your podcast for a limited time period, generally 90 days. Otherwise we work upon all the necessary factors to make your show go viral. If you're interested, please go to www.ViralPodcasting.com/application, complete it and hit submit. I will personally contact you and let you know if I believe we're a good fit. Good luck on your podcasting endeavors and remember Winston Churchill's 10 most important words in the English Language: "Never give up, never give up, never ever give up!"

Appendix

GELLER MEDIA INTERNATIONAL'S CREATING POWERFUL
COMMUNICATOR PRINCIPLES

- Tell the truth.
- Make it matter.
- Never be boring.
- Speak visually, in terms your audience can "picture."
- Start with your best material.
- Address the individual, use "You" — talk to ONE person at a time!
- Do engaging transitions.
- Promote, brag about your stuff.
- Brag about other people's stuff.
- Be who you are on the radio.
- Take risks.
- Dare to be great.

ALWAYS ASK:

- What's in this for me-your listener?
- Is it relevant?
- Does it matter?
- Do you care?
- Can you make the audience care?

*Follow Valerie Geller's guidelines at the end of this book for creating powerful radio.

GELLER MEDIA INTERNATIONALS AIRCHECK CRITERIA

- Are you: Speaking conversationally, directly to each listener?
- READING?
- Sounding as though you are reading?
- Making smooth transitions?
- Are there "brick walls" between the elements or does the presentation feel seamless? Speaking visually?
- Telling powerful stories?
- Introducing the audience to characters they can care about?
- Funny?
- Is there humor?
- Taking the audience on a journey?
- Presenting moments of truth that connect?
- Including what's NEW?
- Including authentic self-revelation? — Do I know you, from this show?
- Going "personal" without going private?
- Boring?
- Did anything go too long?
- Taking risks?
- Any surprises in this show?
- Providing "talkable topics" for your listeners for later in the day to discuss with others?
- If so, what?
- Having fun?
- Giving your audience enough to make them want to come back?
- Serving your listeners? (Entertained, Informed, Inspired, Persuaded, Connected?) Compelling?
- Would your listener sit in a parked car and keep listening?

*Follow Valerie Geller's guidelines at the end of this book for creating powerful radio.

Those Who Can Do!

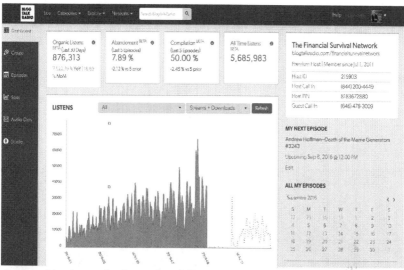

Jason Hartman's Creating Wealth

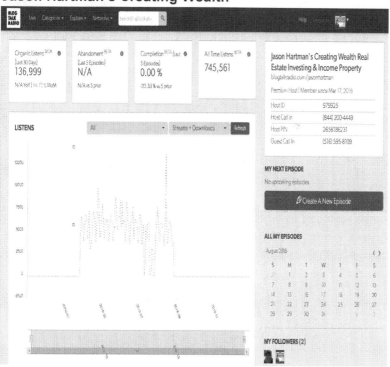

The Golden Rule with David Fischer

General Stats

Total Downloads

Search:

Time Period	Downloads
August	69,665
July	25,656
All Time	95,321

| Page 1 of 1 GO | 10 ⬍ per Page | Now Displaying 1 - 3 of 3 |

⬛ EXPORT

Downloads by Episode

Search:

Title	Creation Date	August	July	June	Total	Action
David Fischer--The Negative Interest Rate Epidemic Show #8	2016-08-23 18:52:27	2	0	0	2	🔎 DETAILS
The Trend Is Your Friend, Or Is It? Show #7	2016-08-16 18:30:13	5,663	0	0	5,663	🔎 DETAILS
David Fischer--Crafting Your Financial Blueprint	2016-08-04 20:16:36	14,441	0	0	14,441	🔎 DETAILS
David Fischer--Post Brexit ALL GOOD!? If Deutsche Bank fails what if? Show #6	2016-07-27 00:29:12	7,127	0	0	7,127	🔎 DETAILS
David Fischer--Converting IRA's To Physical Gold Without Tax Consequences Show #5	2016-07-25 16:11:05	9,076	1	0	9,077	🔎 DETAILS
Show #4 Brexit Aftermath, Deutsche Bank, Monte deo Paschi, Gold's Big Move, Confusion About Gold	2016-07-19 18:44:36	14,707	0	0	14,707	🔎 DETAILS
Show #3- Explaining the Bail-Ins & The Dodd Frank Act	2016-07-13 02:00:14	13,890	4	0	13,894	🔎 DETAILS
Show #2 - Gold 101 Education, Gold's Future, What about Silver?	2016-07-13 01:57:49	4,738	6,345	0	11,083	🔎 DETAILS
Show #1- Brexit-What Happened-How It Affected The Markets, What Does the Future Hold?	2016-07-13 01:40:05	21	19,306	0	19,327	🔎 DETAILS

| Page 1 of 1 GO | 10 ⬍ per Page | Now Displaying 1 - 9 of 9 |

Amazon Show with Mike Gazzola
General Stats

Total Downloads

Search:

Time Period	Downloads ▾
August	70,743
July	4,314
All Time	75,057

| Page 1 of 1 GO | 10 ⬍ per Page | Now Displaying 1 - 3 of 3 |

🖫 EXPORT

Downloads by Episode

Search:

Title	Creation Date	Downloads August	July	June	Total	Action
On the Way to $1 Million in Sales...How Did He Do It? Show #11	2016-08-25 15:57:05	116	0	0	116	🔎 DETAILS
Mike Gazzola – Free Products for the Asking! Show #10	2016-08-18 18:44:37	48	0	0	48	🔎 DETAILS
Amazon--White Labeling vs Retail Arbitrage Show #9	2016-08-11 20:12:46	412	0	0	412	🔎 DETAILS
Mike Gazzola--Still Mining The Amazon Mother Lode	2016-08-05 19:30:44	465	0	0	465	🔎 DETAILS
6 and 7 Figure Incomes On Amazon And How Not To Fail Show #8	2016-08-01 14:32:01	17,348	0	0	17,348	🔎 DETAILS
Mining The Amazon Mother Lode Show #2	2016-07-29 17:45:50	546	0	0	546	🔎 DETAILS
Mike Gazzola – Striking Gold on Amazon.com Show #1	2016-07-29 17:20:25	605	0	0	605	🔎 DETAILS
Where To Get Your Products At The Best Possible Price And Quality Show #7	2016-07-29 14:49:52	16,061	0	0	16,061	🔎 DETAILS
Buying Products At The Right Price And Pricing Them Properly Show #6	2016-07-27 19:27:14	15,109	0	0	15,109	🔎 DETAILS
Getting To The Top Of Amazon Without Spending A Lot #5	2016-07-27 18:32:58	11,715	0	0	11,715	🔎 DETAILS

| Page 1 of 2 GO | 10 ⬍ per Page | Now Displaying 1 - 10 of 11 |

🖫 EXPORT

Podcasts

Library   Unplayed   Store

Top Audio Podcasts

Episodes   Audio Podcasts

Business ⌄

1. Easy Residual Income
Mike...

2. Marketing, Entrepreneurship,...
Lance Tamashiro

3. The Brutal Truth About Sales & Selli..
Brian Burns, B2B Sal...

4. Sales Questions and Brutally Honest...
Brian Burns - Sales S...

5. Planet Money
NPR

6. How I Built This
NPR

7. The Tim Ferriss Show
Tim Ferriss: Bestsell...

8. StartUp Podcast
Gimlet

9. The Dave Ramsey Show
Ramsey Solutions

10. SimpNess: II Podcast che...
Piernicola De Maria

11. P&L With Pimm Fox and Lisa
Bloomberg News

12. Marketplace
Marketplace

13. The Art of Charm | Social Science |...
Jordan Harbinger an...

14. The Ziglar Show - Inspiring Your True...
Inspiration and Itung...

15. Jocko Podcast
Jocko Podcast

16. EOFire | Entrepreneur on Fi...
John Lee Dumas: Ent...

17. The EntreLeadership
Ramsey Solutions

18. BiggerPockets Podcast : Real Esta...
BiggerPockets.com ·...

Podcasts

Library Unplayed Store

Top Audio Podcasts

Episodes Audio Podcasts

All Categories ∨

1. Easy Residual Income
Mike

2. The Axe Files with David Axelrod
CNN

3. The Scumbag!
Ed Zitron and Felix Bi...

4. This American Life
This American Life

5. Sancit Holistic Podcast
Aron O'Dowd

6. Marketing, Entrepreneurship,...
Lance Tamashiro

7. Lore
Aaron Mahnke

8. The Brutal Truth About Sales & Selli...
Brian Burns, B2B Sel...

9. TED Radio Hour
NPR

10. Sales Questions and Brutally Honest...
Brian Burns - Sales S...

11. Radiolab
WNYC Studios

12. Stuff You Should Know
HowStuffWorks.com

13. The Joe Rogan Experience
Joe Rogan

14. Planet Money
NPR

15. Revisionist History
Malcolm Gladwell / P...

16. NPR Politics Podcast
NPR

17. How I Built This
NPR

18. Serial
This American Life

19. Kickass News

20. Freakonomics

21. Fresh Air

22. Hannibal Buress:

23. FiveThirtyEight

24. Dan Carlin's

MOBI Business Plan Template

Once you decide to go into business, it's natural to feel a sense of urgency to start selling. Yet, the most overlooked step to starting a successful business is creating a business plan. Your business plan provides a map of the future. It is a key tool in discovery, process, and strategic planning. By creating a business plan, you are writing the narrative of your small business and will be able to clearly share your vision with potential investors, new employees and suppliers.

The MOBI Business Plan template consists of 15 sections that correspond directly to the content of Course 1: Starting a Business. We suggest completing each section of the business plan after you complete the correlating session in the course. This business plan is a universal model suitable for all types of business, which you can customize to fit your circumstances. MOBI provides leading topics, questions and suggestions in each section to guide you.

1. On the cover page replace the MOBI spark with your own logo and provide your business name, personal name and date.
2. Complete each section using the suggestions and questions as guidance. You can type directly over the provided content or delete it as you complete it.
3. The sections will stay separated by page breaks so that your document is well-formatted.

Once you complete your business plan, be sure that key stakeholders review it. Business plans are not static; they will change as your business and the business environment changes around you.

Available as free download at www.scu.edu.mobi

Made in the USA
Charleston, SC
03 February 2017